Endorsements for *Force for Good*

"*Force for Good* is a celebration of sound Catholic ideas as applied to business. The integration of faith and reason enables the Catholic mind to see business in a whole new light, a light that shines on the people-centered approach to building organizations of integrity outlined in Engelland's book. This is a must-read for all faith-filled leaders."

— **Andrew Abela, provost**, The Catholic University of America

"This book is an excellent resource for business professionals who want to understand how they can succeed responsibly while being faithful to the rich heritage of Catholic social teaching."

— **Richard Banziger**, bank executive and consultant

"An incredibly informative and entertaining read! Current and future leaders of all faiths will gain a clear understanding of the positive outcomes that integrity-driven decision-making and behavior bring to a business. Engelland combines sound advice with personal anecdotes and truths of faith to create a roadmap for sustainable business and personal success. Well done! Bravo!"

— **Andrew Gatto**, former CEO, Russ Berrie and Company

"There's a tremendous need for this book, especially now, when so many corporations are struggling to act responsibly. Business leaders want to do the right thing, but many don't know where to begin. Engelland outlines how to infuse integrity into every part of the business. His advice is practical, concise, and right on target."

— **Charlie Reese**, director of mergers and acquisitions (retired), IBM

"There's a lack of engagement from millennials in today's economy because they don't buy into gluttonous consumerism. *Force for Good* is timely in presenting a more authentic approach to economic interaction. This fresh approach uses principles of Catholic Social Teaching to place the customer experience and meaningful jobs as top priorities. Capital gets a fair return but not at the expense of customers and employees. Such an approach should resonate with those entering the workforce and do wonders for the business world."

— **Gellert Dornay**, president and CEO, Axia Home Loans

"Many practical people have forgotten that ethics is an integral part of all human activity, including business. As a result, democratic capitalism is suffering a crisis of moral confidence. This book is a clear, concise, and necessary reminder of some timeless truths. It's a perfect gift for ethically challenged businesspeople and those who love them!"

— **Kishore Jayabalan**, director, Istituto Acton, Rome

"Engelland captures the reader's interest right away. His description of ethical standards as an 'owner's manual' can resonate with any generation. His motivating description of profit as a common ground, much like breathing, that is only the substrate from which a fulfilling desire to 'be good at what you do' rises, calls his readers to strive for greatness that is measured in deeper terms than how much money one makes. This parallels what my years in the military revealed about heroism: a soldier's pay, though necessary to feed his or her family, is way behind patriotism and camaraderie as a motivating influence. This work has the potential to inspire similarly heroic business ventures and behavior, allowing its practitioners to make a real and lasting contribution to society."

— **Fr. Patrick Dolan**, brigadier general (retired), U.S. Army National Guard

"Brian Engelland has published the ideal book for businesspeople who want to be successful and good Christians at the same time. He has done a wonderful job combining stories, which present inspiring role models, with deep theoretical underpinnings that take you through Catholic moral teaching applied to business. I highly recommend the book to all practitioners who wish to be mindful in their actions."

— **Fr. Martin Schlag**, professor for Catholic Social Thought, holder of the Alan W. Moss endowed Chair for Catholic Social Thought at the Center for Catholic Studies, University of St. Thomas (Minnesota), director of the John A. Ryan Institute for Catholic Social Thought

"*Force for Good* uniquely provides pragmatic approaches for establishing integrity throughout organizations. Engelland, importantly, underscores that organizations of trust and integrity spring from a fundamental respect for the human person and are rooted in ethics based on immutable truths and time-tested virtuous behaviors of human morality. Outstanding!"

— **Lawrence J. Blanford**, CEO (retired), Green Mountain Coffee Roasters, Inc.

"Every entrepreneur should read this book — whether you are starting a company, looking to make improvements in your growing company, or reestablishing some of the foundations you thought you would never forget when you created your company long ago. This is a thorough guide to keeping your company on track to qualitative and quantitative profit and, more importantly, to be a true force for good in the world today."

— **Christine Rich**, co-owner and CEO, My Saint My Hero

"*Force for Good* is a persuasive, inspiring, timely message. When integrity is placed in the center of everything, businesses succeed and people flourish. This is a useful guide for all business leaders."

— **Elizabeth Bryant**, vice president, Southwest Airlines University

"The organization of *Force for Good* is masterful. Engelland takes the reader's hand, engages the reader's mind, and then wins over the reader's heart in a compelling narrative that weaves Catholic understanding of the human person into effective management practices. Everyone who reads this book will understand the why and the how of building organizations of integrity."

— **Chris Veno**, principal, Trion Group

"The integral approach to business ethics outlined in this book makes it an excellent guide for business leaders and business students alike. Even experienced businesspeople need continued guidance and education in order to make appropriate ethical decisions for their companies, their employees, and their bottom line. *Force for Good* provides a thorough, integral approach to implementing ethical leadership in the work place."

— **Timothy R. Busch, J.D., CPA**, CEO, Pacific Hospitality Group

"*Force for Good* opens up and explores the wonderful integration that is possible when the vocation to business, and the creation of wealth, are nurtured within the riches of Catholic Social Teaching. Those seeking to discover this transcendent dimension of what is too often regarded as a mere worldly pursuit will profit from this fine work."

— **Frank Hanna**, CEO, Hanna Capital

Force for Good

BRIAN ENGELLAND

FORCE FOR GOOD

The Catholic Guide to Business Integrity

SOPHIA INSTITUTE PRESS
Manchester, New Hampshire

To the eight wonderfully curious people who call me Grandpa: Eva, Malachi, William, Augustine, Gabriel, Sophia, Maximus, and Vivian. May each of them grow in holiness and become a force for good in this world.

Contents

Acknowledgments

This book is a further development of a previous work, *Ethics Essentials for Business Leaders*, which I co-authored with William D. (Denny) Eshee.[1] The last two chapters of this new book are substantially based upon the previous book.

I want to thank my Busch School colleagues who gave me support, encouragement, and ideas during the writing, especially Andrew Abela, Bill Bowman, Bob Keith, Michael Pakaluk, Harvey Seegers, Max Torres, Mark Weber, Andreas Widmer, and Jack Yoest. In addition, I'd like to acknowledge the inspiration I've received from some great business leaders who have supported our school's work, including Tim Busch, Art Ciocca, Edward Pryzbyla, Larry Blanford, Steve Means, and Charles Koch.

I want to thank my children and grandchildren, who kept asking what I was doing (and why!). I also want to thank my loving wife, Barbara, who helped make sure that I kept on task but didn't let the writing become an all-encompassing endeavor.

---

[1] Brian Engelland and William Eshee, *Ethics Essentials for Business Leaders* (Rockville Centre, NY: Sophia Omni Press, 2011).

Force for Good

Finally, I want to thank God and the intercession of Venerable Fulton J. Sheen, for curing my cancer and giving me the time and inspiration to complete this project.

Force for Good

Introduction

The four of us were about to capture the American dream. We had just signed paperwork to begin a time-phased buyout of a large manufacturing company. Of course, the business had some big problems, or else it wouldn't have been for sale. It was a private-label manufacturer with a limited product line, no real branding, no distribution system, little cash, antiquated technology, and a union contract that kept the company from adding labor-saving improvements.

But we were undeterred. One of us was a marketing expert who knew how to introduce new products, build brands, and grow distribution. Another was a manufacturing guru who knew how to fine-tune equipment to get optimal performance. The third was a financial whiz, and the fourth was adept at HR and working with unions. Our vision was to create a business that overcame the short-term mentality of the major companies we had worked for. We wanted to run this business in the right way, a way that developed customer loyalty and commitment. And we had assembled the right team to get the job done.

Well, we thought we did.

Unfortunately, we didn't first agree on a list of principles for our new firm. As we took the initial steps needed to fix the business, we quickly learned that we had no margin for error. To make the monthly cash-flow numbers to keep the banks happy, we found that we had to apply a short-term mentality to decisions, the same mentality we disliked when we were working for large corporations. When our financial expert and my two team members recommended what I considered unethical bank reporting, I realized that it was time for me to leave.

So, you might be asking yourself, "Why should I read a book about integrity written by someone who failed to convince three friends that values are important to running a business?"

My answer is … "scar tissue." When I look at my limbs, I can see several reminders of mistakes I've made. I have a scar on one finger from not being careful with a pocket knife. I got the scar on my thumb from trying to work on a clock without first removing the tension from the main spring. The two scars on my shin? I have those because I wasn't careful climbing on some playground equipment as a child. I also have mental scars from failures over the years. Scars can help us remember mistakes and learn from them so that we avoid making the same mistake again. When you read this book, you can learn from my "scars."

Force for Good arose out of a career-long interest in doing the right thing and doing it in the right way. My thinking is profoundly influenced by my parents. My dad grew up on a large Kansas farm, where he learned that equipment serves an important function at planting and harvest time. It must be properly maintained if it is to be useful when needed. Later he applied that understanding in developing a residential heating and air conditioning business. My mom was a kindergarten teacher and had great skill in using stories to explain things in simple terms. She had a compelling way of establishing order and demonstrating purpose in everyday activities. She had a joy for life that was contagious.

Introduction

My two-stage career benefited by my practicing the skills modeled by my parents, first as a product development specialist and later as a college professor. In the first stage, I learned what must be done to create market-leading products and services that inspire customers to buy. In the second, I learned that students want to know not only what works, but also why. The why is very important. By knowing the why, we can adapt more effectively when conditions change.

I've written this book with both business practitioners and business students in mind, and I've tried to structure the writing so that I explain not only what works but why it works. Further, I've tried to keep the writing crisp and to the point, and I've added examples to illustrate the ideas presented. I hope you'll agree that this makes the book readable and interesting.

There's a great need for integrity in business these days. Business leaders, employees, consumers, and the general public are tired of the old "business as usual" formula that pushes mediocre products to consumers at outlandish prices. Everyone is reaching the same conclusion. Trust is the glue that holds business together, and where there is no trust, there can be no business. Operating with integrity is the only way to develop and maintain trusting relationships over the long haul.

And integrity is a compelling term. The term resonates with most business people and helps capture what is needed to achieve good results. Yet most of the books and articles written about integrity fail to specify how to implement it across the organization. The reader is left to create his or her own implementation approach, and that can be a hit-or-miss endeavor.

In this book, I explain how integrity is established so that every aspect of the business is conducted consistently using one set of standards. The first chapter sets forth necessary terminology.

The second provides the natural law foundation that is required for establishing trusting relationships in business. Chapter 3 explains the four core principles from Catholic Social Doctrine (CSD) that allow human interaction in business to achieve its full potential. The fourth chapter describes the importance of virtue and in creating the proper environment for integrity. Chapters 5 through 7 provide guidance on achieving integrity-infused relationships with employees, customers, and the rest of society. Finally, chapters 8 and 9 provide a step-by-step approach for implementing integrity in one's business.

The title of this book is borrowed from the tagline "business as a force for good," which was adopted by the Catholic University of America's school of business and economics at its founding. The phrase harkens to comments that Pope Leo XIII wrote in his 1891 encyclical *Rerum Novarum* about how employers should look out for the common good of workers.[2] Pope Leo is an inspirational figure for our school. He is the pope who signed the charter that began the Catholic University of America, and his encyclical led to the establishment of a department for the study of economics, which later became our Busch School of Business and Economics.

Pope Leo understood the struggle between good and evil and wrote the popular prayer that begins "St. Michael the Archangel, defend us in battle, be our protection against the wickedness and snares of the devil." Michael is the angel who drove Lucifer out of heaven, and artists have portrayed him as an imposing figure, dressed in battle armor, shield, and sword. His image offers great inspiration for the business person who strives to make his or her business a force for good.

---

[2] Leo XIII (1891) encyclical *Rerum Novarum*, May 15, 1891, no. 20.

Chapter 1

Doing Business the Right Way

*Right is right even if nobody is right, and wrong
is wrong even if everyone is wrong.*[3]

—Fulton J. Sheen

Integrity. When we think about individuals with integrity, we think of people who have a consistent commitment to honor moral, ethical, spiritual, and artistic values.[4] When we apply the word to engineering design, we think of the ability of a structure to hold together under a load, resisting breakage or bending.[5]

But when we think about integrity in business organizations, we combine the two so that we look at values *and* structure. If we want to build a business with lasting integrity, we need to define the values we hold dear as an organization and develop a structure that maintains those values over the long term, even in

[3] Fulton J. Sheen, *Thoughts for Daily Living* (Garden City, NY: Garden City, 1955), p. 139.
[4] Barbara Killinger, *Integrity: Doing the Right Thing for the Right Reason* (Montreal: McGill-Queen's University Press, 2010), p. 12.
[5] Andrew E. Samuel and John Weir, *Introduction to Engineering Design: Modelling, Synthesis, and Problem Solving Strategies* (Burlington, MA: Elsevier, 1999), pp. 2–10.

the face of adversity. This requires clearly developed core values, defined principles, controls, and the building of a culture that is reflected in day-to-day practice.[6]

Yes, there's a right way to do things, and that's what integrity is all about. There are no shortcuts. If you want your business to operate in the right way, then you've come to the right place. Creating an ethical business organization built on integrity is an important undertaking that will require attention, planning, and hard work. This book is intended to be your guide along the way.

If you go whitewater rafting, you want your guide to tell you not only what to do but also why to do it that way. Without the why, some of us in the raft would likely not understand the importance of each action. This could result in inattention to important details and in taking shortcuts that could end in disaster. My intent with this book is to serve as such a guide — to provide you not only with the what, but also with the why.

As we get started, there are a couple of concepts I'd like us to agree on before we start digging into the details of business integrity. On the next few pages I'd like to bring you along to an understanding of what we mean by "good" business, business as a calling, business ethics, and the key problems in ethics education that challenge all of us.

What do we mean by "good" business?

The word "good" has at least two meanings when applied to business. It can refer to the *quantity* of business activity and indicate

---

[6] D. Christopher Kayes, David Stirling, and Tjai M. Nielsen, "Building Organizational Integrity," *Business Horizons* 50, no. 1 (January-February 2007): 61–70.

that activity levels are sufficient and substantial, better than merely average. It can also refer to the *quality* of business, in the sense that what is happening is beneficial to a broader expanse of society, not just the owners. The latter understanding of "good" has generated substantial interest in recent years and has resulted in numerous books and articles on the topic. Three books by CEOs illustrate my point.

In *Good Returns*, George Schwartz of Ave Maria Mutual Funds presented his ideas about making money through morally responsible investing. He described good returns as "achieving religiously endorsed investment objectives while not entangling you in morally questionable business practices."[7] In *Conscious Capitalism*, John Mackey of Whole Foods Markets described the "good" in business as serving others effectively, so that the quality of their lives is improved.[8] In *Good Profit*, Charles Koch of Koch Industries wrote, "Good profit comes from Principled Entrepreneurship — creating superior value for our customers while consuming fewer resources and always acting lawfully and with integrity. Good profit comes from making a contribution in society — not from corporate welfare or other ways of taking advantage of people."[9]

Judging by what these three CEOs have to say, an important meaning of "good" encompasses moral responsibility, serving

---

[7] George P. Schwartz, *Good Returns: Making Money by Morally Responsible Investing* (Ann Arbor, MI: Geodi Publishing, 2010), p. xv.

[8] John Mackey and Raj Sisodia, *Liberating the Heroic Spirit of Business: Conscious Capitalism* (Boston, MA: Harvard Business Review Press, 2013), pp. 61–64.

[9] Charles G. Koch, *Good Profit: How Creating Value for Others Built One of the World's Most Successful Companies* (New York: Crown Business, 2015), p. 4.

others, and making an authentic contribution to society. A morally good business "attends to the goods proper to it as a specialized association and employs ethically sound means to achieve those goods."[10]

Increasingly, both quantitative and qualitative dimensions of "good" business are valued by business leaders and society. But can businesses achieve both at the same time? Or does striving for success in quality reduce the success in quantity?

The evidence indicates not only that businesses can be successful in both but also that success in the qualitative dimension often leads to success in the quantitative dimension. This is because treating employees, customers, and society at large with compassion and respect helps to build brand loyalty and repeat business. People appreciate valuable products, fair prices, and responsive, friendly service and tend to support businesses that provide these things.[11]

The Catholic perspective has long recognized the importance of the qualitative side of business. In his 1931 encyclical *Quadragesimo Anno*, Pope Pius XI warned that morality can't be allowed to be subverted by an economic system ruled solely by competitive forces.[12] Social justice and social charity demands that individuals and governments who participate in the economy must act to uphold morality. Oswald von Nell-Breuning,

---

[10] Robert G. Kennedy, *The Good That Business Does* (Grand Rapids, MI: Acton Institute, 2006), p. 68.

[11] Arjun Chaudhuri and Morris Holbrook, "The Chain of Effects from Brand Trust and Brand Affect to Brand Performance: The Role of Brand Loyalty," *Journal of Marketing* 65, no. 2 (2001): 81–93.

[12] Pius XI, Encyclical Letter *Quadragesimo Anno* (May 15, 1931), no. 88.

one of the theologians who helped write *Quadragesimo Anno*, described the good entrepreneur as one who

> gives first thought to service and second thought to gain; ... employs workingmen for the creation of goods of true worth; ... does not wrong them by demanding that they take part in the creation of futilities, or even harmful and evil things; ... and offers to the consumer nothing but useful goods and services rather than, taking advantage of the latter's inexperience or weakness, betrays him into spending his money for things he does not need, or [products] that are not only useless but even injurious to him.[13]

Successful businesses can be exciting places to work. Through innovation, creativity, and initiative, they examine human needs and bring entirely new products to life. But those products need to contribute effectively to the common good by serving authentic needs.

When I was growing up, my father ran a residential heating and cooling contracting business, and I accompanied him on a service call to one of the wealthier families in our community. I was too young to do any work other than carrying tools in from the truck. My dad examined the heating system to determine what was wrong and then told the homeowner, "The thermocouple is shot. It'll set you back about twenty-five dollars to replace it."

The homeowner then asked how much my dad would charge to replace the whole heating and cooling system. "But you don't need a new one," my dad said.

---

[13] Oswald von Nell-Breuning, *Reorganization of Social Economy* (Milwaukee: Bruce, 1936), pp. 115–116.

The man replied, "Well, I replace my car every year with a new one. Why shouldn't I replace my heating and cooling system?"

"Furnaces and air conditioners have fewer moving parts and are built to last much longer than a car," explained my dad. And he refused to give the man a price.

On the way home, I asked my dad why he wouldn't sell the man a new system. My dad turned to me and said, "It's not right to sell someone something he doesn't need. That furnace of his will last another fifteen years, and the money it would cost for a new one could be put to much better use. He could save it for a rainy day, take his wife on vacation, or pay for his children's education."

I don't know whether the customer went to a competitor and bought a new system or spent his money on something else. But I do know that my dad earned a sterling reputation for honesty and fair dealing throughout the community. He conveyed a sense of value that customers admired. As a result, he never seemed to lack for business.

Pope Leo XIII explained this relationship well in his 1891 encyclical, *Rerum Novarum*. He wrote that, under conditions where businesses meet human needs and "Christian morality, when adequately and completely practiced, leads of itself to temporal prosperity."[14] My dad's cultivation of a solid ethical reputation helped him attract repeat business year after year. People knew that they would get a fair deal, and they knew that he wouldn't sell them something just so he could increase his own income.

---

[14] Leo XIII (1891), Encyclical Letter *Rerum Novarum* (May 15, 1891), no. 28.

Presumably, he could have sold many more new heating and cooling systems than he did, but if, by spending money on new furnaces needlessly, people had less money to spend on necessities, the community might be less well off. Pope Benedict expressed this negative potential when he wrote, "But should profit become the exclusive goal of the enterprise, the business risks destroying true wealth and creating poverty for all concerned."[15] Foolish expenditures impoverish consumers even though they might benefit the seller.

What is the real goal of business?

Many people today are under the mistaken impression that the goal of business is always to maximize profits. Where did this false notion get started? Some blame Adam Smith, the founder of modern economics, who, in explaining economic principles in his book *An Inquiry into the Wealth of Nations*, wrote, "It is not from the benevolence of the butcher, the brewer, or the baker that we expect our dinner, but from their regard to their own interest."[16] "Own interest" is taken by some to be shorthand for "maximum profits."

More contemporary scholars have echoed this idea. For instance, when Milton Friedman was asked whether corporate executives have responsibilities other than making as much money for their stockholders as possible, he referred to Adam Smith and said, "There is one and only one social responsibility of

---

[15] Benedict XVI, Encyclical Letter *Caritas in Veritate* (June 29, 2009), no. 21.

[16] Adam Smith, *An Inquiry into the Wealth of Nations* (1776; repr., New York: Bantam Dell, 2003), pp. 23–24.

business — to use its resources and engage in activities designed to increase its profits."[17]

But there's another way in which scholars interpret Adam Smith's insight. You see, Smith authored a prior book, *The Theory of Moral Sentiments*, in which he provided the ethical, philosophical, psychological, and methodological underpinnings of *The Wealth of Nations*. In this earlier book, Smith explained his idea of "own interest" as being good at what we do because being good leads to our individual happiness.[18] Attempting to be good at what we do might involve the butcher's providing the best cut of meat, the brewer's brewing the finest beer, or the baker's baking the most delicious loaf of bread. Being good is a much different idea than attempting to maximize the spread between income and expense. So, attributing the idea of profit maximization to Adam Smith is considered by some as a gross simplification of his basic idea.

Certainly, profits are important — you can't remain in business very long without them — and they provide a good indication of whether a business is functioning well. Firms that focus first on profit, however, often miss the little things that can make their business better able to create superior value for customers. In a successful business, the ethical treatment of employees and customers is the first priority. As St. John Paul II wrote, the purpose of business is not simply to make a profit, but rather to create a community of persons that produces something good to serve

[17] Milton Friedman, *Capitalism and Freedom* (Chicago: University of Chicago Press, 1962), p. 133.

[18] Adam Smith, *The Theory of Moral Sentiments*, ed. D. D. Raphael and A. L. Macfie (1759; repr., Oxford: 1976 Oxford University Press, 1976), part VI.

the needs of society.[19] Serving others is the principle concern of business. Serving others well is the ultimate goal.

What about greed?

In the hit movie *Wall Street*, the character Michael Douglas plays makes an impassioned speech in defense of greed. He says, "Greed is good. Greed is right. Greed works. Greed clarifies, cuts through, and captures the essence of the evolutionary spirit. Greed in all its forms—greed for life, for money, for love, for knowledge—has marked the upward surge of mankind."

Greed certainly played a large role in the housing market crash of 2008,[20] and corporate greed may be an element in many of the ethical issues we read about in the news.[21] But to say that greed has marked the upward surge of mankind or that all corporations are greedy is a gross mischaracterization.

Spurred on by Hollywood, the general public exhibits a pronounced misunderstanding of the profit motive that is part of corporate DNA. I often hear complaints that big companies care only about making money and, by their nature, don't care about employees, customers, or the needs of society at large. This misconception is reinforced by news reporting that focuses on

---

[19] John Paul II, Encyclical *Centesimus Annus* (May 1, 1991), no. 35.

[20] Donald T. Wargo, Norman Baglini, and Kate Nelson (2009), "The Global Financial Crisis Caused by Greed, Moral Meltdown, and Public Policy Disasters," *Forum on Public Policy: A Journal of the Oxford Round Table* 2009, no. 1.

[21] Mathew T. Clements, "Self-Interest vs. Greed and the Limitations of the Invisible Hand," *American Journal of Economics and Sociology* 72, no. 4 (2013).

A New Paradigm for Business

Imagine a business that is born out of a dream about how the world could be and should be ... one that aspires to so much more than making money ... a force for good that enhances the health and well-being of society ... a business that enriches the world by its existence, and brings joy, fulfillment, and a sense of meaning to all who are touched by it.

Picture a business built on love and care rather than stress and fear, whose team members are passionate and committed to their work ... and who find themselves at the end of each day newly inspired and freshly committed to what brought them to the business in the first place, the opportunity to be a part of something larger than themselves, to make a difference, to craft a purposeful life while earning a living.

Think about a business that cares profoundly about the well-being of its customers, seeing them not as

corporate greed rather than on the good that businesses do.[22] Some media outlets project the attitude that profit is a four-letter word and when profits increase, it must mean that someone is getting the shaft—customers, employees, or the general

[22] Sheena Raja, "A Crippling Sin: An Exploration of 'Greed' in Global News Magazine Discourse," *Global Media Journal* (June 2014).

consumers but as flesh-and-blood human beings whom it is privileged to serve.

Envision a business that embraces outsiders as insiders, inviting its suppliers into the family circle and treating them with the same love and care it showers on customers and team members.

Imagine a business that exists in a virtuous cycle of multifaceted value creation, generating social, intellectual, emotional, spiritual, cultural, physical, and ecological wealth and well-being for everyone it touches.

Such businesses are not imaginary entities in some fictional utopia. They exist in the real world, by the dozens today, but soon by the hundreds and thousands.*

*This description is taken from John Mackey and Raj Sisodia, *Conscious Capitalism: Liberating the Historic Spirit of Business* (Boston: Harvard Business Review Press, 2014), p. 31. John Mackey is co-CEO of Whole Food Markets.

public. Look at some recent headline examples: "Energy Suppliers Pocket Biggest Profit Margins in Two Years as Households Suffer," "Banks Cut Services to Maintain Profits," and "Cash Grab by Big Business."

This anti-profit attitude doesn't consider that failing businesses don't create new products and services, don't hire new employees, and don't create economic well-being. Only profitable businesses do. So when businesses announce news regarding improved profitability, it is not a bad thing. In fact, it's usually a good thing.

But maintaining that businesses exist to generate profits is like saying that the only obligation of a human person is to breathe air. Sure, profits are necessary for business survival, just as breathing is necessary for human survival. But profits or breathing are not the only necessities. Humans exist to accomplish a host of important objectives, including working, forming loving relationships, raising families, and becoming more complete as a result. Similarly, businesses seek to accomplish many objectives, including the creation of high-quality products, the service of customers, and the fair treatment of employees. Granted, profitability is needed, or the firm will not survive for long. But profit is more of a scorekeeping discipline than a driving force. St. John Paul II said it well:

> Profit is a regulator of the life of a business, but it is not the only one; other human and moral factors must also be considered which, in the long run, are at least equally important for the life of a business.[23]

Businesses serve an important and irreplaceable role in this world. They create products and perform services that individuals or government bodies are ill-equipped to provide. These products and services make the transportation, education, housing, food, and healthcare challenges of life easier to bear.

Today, the business leaders I know run their organizations to address the needs and desires of consumers, employees, suppliers, and the communities in which their businesses are located. Their daily concerns involve product quality, new-product

---

[23] John Paul II, *Centesimus Annus*, no. 35.

innovation, employee training, and supplier partnerships, to name a few. Those businesses that achieve success in these areas usually achieve consistent profitability. But there is an important chain of causality here. Profits arise not because they are the overriding goal but because of a focus on all of the individual, people-related elements of running a business that involve building trusting relationships with everyone involved.

When we reduce the content of business to a summary performance metric such as profits, we can miss the soul of the business: its people. Putting people first tends to yield a prosperity that enables the business to continue.[24] Businesses exist to serve people with products, services, jobs, and the necessities of life. When businesses do well in accomplishing those objectives, investors earn a return on their investment, and that return is called profit. This is not greed.

Is business a calling?

When Pope Francis spoke to the U.S. Congress in September 2015, he repeated a statement he had made on several occasions. He proclaimed, "Business is a noble vocation," and went on to say that the free-enterprise system plays an important role in helping solve the problems of this world. What does he mean by "noble vocation"? We normally talk about priests and nuns who have a vocation. Certainly, he can't be speaking about business from a religious perspective, can he?

Actually, Pope Francis is quoting from a document published in 2012 by the Pontifical Council of Justice and Peace that

---

[24] Leo XIII, *Rerum Novarum*, no. 28.

assures us that business is a vocation, a calling from God.[25] The document suggests that God gives each of us talents, interests, and yearnings of the heart. When we discern with prayer, we can recognize if we are being called to the business profession in which we commit our lives to serving others and to help make the world's products and services more readily available to everyone.

If business is a calling and not a job, then that changes our perspective completely. A job is something we do to make money so we can spend our time on what we really want to do, such as play golf, go to the theater, or take a vacation. We want to minimize the time spent working the job while maximizing the pay we receive in return. But a calling is our overriding mission in life, how we contribute to the world, and what we want to devote all of our best efforts to. If God is calling us to do something, we want to do it well, very well. And for someone so motivated, a career in business becomes that person's lifelong joy!

My own choice of career illustrates this idea. When I was young, I wanted to emulate my father and my grandfather. Both were entrepreneurs. My grandfather studied engineering in college and invented a device that would convert the old-style manual-feed coal furnace into a gas-fired furnace. He set up a manufacturing plant to produce these units and sold them to dealers throughout the Midwest. My father studied business in college, and when he took over my grandfather's business, he expanded operations to create a heating and cooling service capability and installed and serviced new systems all over northern

---

[25] Peter K. A. Turkson and Mario Toso, *Vocation of the Business Leader: A Reflection* (Vatican City: Pontifical Council for Justice and Peace, 2013).

Ohio. My natural abilities seemed to draw me toward either engineering or business, but I needed some guidance in making a good career choice.

I remember seeing televised reports of President John F. Kennedy's May 4, 1961, address to Congress in which he outlined the U.S. commitment to travel to the moon. In his speech, he stated, "I believe that this nation should commit itself to achieving the goal, before this decade is out, of landing a man on the moon and returning him safely to the earth."[26] The space race had begun.

The challenge of going to the moon captivated my attention. I took extra science and math classes in high school and went on to Purdue to study engineering. In retrospect, my interests and abilities, combined with significant current events that captured my imagination, seemed to be God's way of propelling me toward my initial career in engineering. Later, my success in engineering drew me into business, and my success there encouraged my further education and eventual second career as a college professor. Was all this coincidence, or did I receive heavenly guidance? Pope Francis's reference to business as a vocation suggests the latter.

Routinely I encourage students to analyze their innate abilities and distinctive interests and then look toward careers that utilize those abilities and interests. The world needs people who are good at what they do, not people drawn to a job just because they can earn a living doing it.

Many business schools promote enrollment by touting the job opportunities and pay levels of business graduates. Earn a

---

[26] See John F. Kennedy, "Excerpt from the 'Special Message to the Congress on Urgent National Needs,' posted on the website of NASA, May 24, 2004, https://www.nasa.gov/.

Orville and Wilbur Wright: Just Flyers or Good Businessmen?

Most everyone knows that the Wright brothers were the first to build and fly a powered aircraft, but very few know that in addition to being inventors, both were highly ethical businessmen. But they started out only reluctantly.

In fact, Wilbur didn't like business at all. After working in Orville's printing business and then helping Orville start a bicycle shop, he wrote the following analysis: "In business, it is the aggressive man who continually has his eye on his own interest who succeeds. No man has ever been successful in business who was not aggressive, self-assertive, and even a little bit selfish perhaps.... I entirely agree that the boys of the Wright family are all lacking in determination and push. That is the very reason that none of us have been or will be more than ordinary businessmen."*

Back in the late 1800s, *caveat emptor* or "let the buyer beware" was the norm for business. But the brothers implemented a different, more customer-oriented strategy. By providing customers with fair dealing, liberal terms, and the safe products that customers wanted, the Wright brothers' bicycle business grew and grew.

*David McCullough (2015), *The Wright Brothers* (New York: Simon and Schuster, 2015), p. 24.

This formula for success also worked very well in the airplane business. The brothers organized their research, product development, and flight demonstrations, all with an eye to providing excellent value to their customers. Unlike competitors who skirted patents while pushing the bounds of safety, the Wrights operated a customer-oriented business. As a result, they made powered flight a safe undertaking that accelerated its acceptance as a legitimate form of transportation, and achieved fame and fortune as a result. We are all the beneficiaries of their business approach.

business degree if you want to make a lot of money, they say. This approach may sound practical, but it reinforces the moneymaking aspects of business while downplaying the service aspects. By using this pitch, business schools can end up attracting students who come to the profession because of a love of money instead of a love of others. At the end of the day, business is about serving others well. Most of those who choose business because of a love for money will ultimately be disappointed with their choice.

The practice of business offers so much more to the individual worker in terms of challenge, excitement, relationships, and authentic service. As St. John Paul II wrote, those who work not only accomplish the task at hand, but they themselves become more than what they were before the work began.[27] Work can

[27] John Paul II, Encyclical Letter *Laborem Exercens*, September 14, 1981, no. 9.

provide outstanding subjective benefits. When one accepts a calling to business generously and faithfully, a new world of possibilities opens up.

What is business ethics?

In baseball, the umpire watches each pitch and calls it a ball or a strike, depending on whether the ball passes through an imaginary zone defined by the official rules of major league baseball. The lower boundary of the zone is the hollow below the batter's kneecaps; the upper boundary is the midpoint between the batter's waist and shoulders, and the side boundaries are the outside edges of home plate. Umpires are evaluated by the league as to how well they consistently apply these boundaries in making their calls. Still, there tends to be some variation in calls due to the difficulty of judging the path of a thrown baseball. Disagreements arise, and some players are ejected for arguing the ump's call.

Baseball gives umpires clear guidelines for judging. Not so ethics, where there is often even disagreement about what should be judged and how to judge it. Many people possess different understandings of ethics and even use a different frame of reference. This problem begins with the definition of the term.

His Excellency Tadeusz Kondrusiewicz, the archbishop of Minsk, told me the following story. After the fall of communism in the Soviet Union, many people began taking courses to learn Western-style business practices. In once such class, the professor was asked to explain business ethics. "It's like this," he said. "Suppose that a sight-impaired woman comes into the grocery shop to buy some things. She makes a selection and is told that she owes 1,000 rubles. She searches in her purse and pulls out what she thinks are two 500-ruble banknotes and hands them to the clerk, but in reality they are two 5,000-ruble notes. This is where business ethics comes in, because the clerk is faced with a difficult ethical decision. Should he pocket the extra 9,000 rubles for himself? Or should he give half of them to his boss?"

All joking aside, some have defined ethics as rules adopted by organizations to guide behavior. For instance, the best-selling business ethics text states that "ethics comprises organizational principles, values, and norms that may originate from individuals, organizational statements, or from the legal system and that primarily guide individual or group behavior."[28]

Some books treat ethics as a process for making decisions about which action might be better in a given situation. One leading book states that "ethics refers to our efforts to figure out what we should do and how we should live. More specifically, it involves the challenge of figuring out how to justify our behavior both to ourselves and others."[29] Others suggest that ethics is neither rules nor procedures *per se*; instead, it comprises the study of how personal moral standards influence organizational behavior.[30]

All of these definitions imply that each organization will likely adopt different ethical standards because no objective universal ethical standard is available. This is a problem.

---

[28] O. C. Ferrell, John Fraedrich, and Linda Ferrell, *Business Ethics: Ethical Decision Making and Cases*, 10th edition (Stamford, CT: Cengage Learning, 2015), p. 5.

[29] Andrew C. Wicks, R. Edward Freeman, Patricia H. Werhane, and Kirsten E. Martin, *Business Ethics: A Managerial Approach* (Upper Saddle River, NJ: Prentice Hall, 2010), p. 4.

[30] Laura L. Nash, *Good Intentions Aside: A Manager's Guide to Resolving Ethical Problems* (Boston: Harvard Business School Press, 1993), p. 5.

Using any of these definitions is like throwing out the baseball rulebook and telling each umpire to implement his own idea regarding what he might consider a strike. Any of these definitions could be used by the Nazi Third Reich to show that the Nazis were an ethical organization. After all, the Nazis did study ethics, adopt rules of conduct, and implement procedures for deciding what should be done. If the definition we use for ethics makes the Nazi regime look ethical, then we've got a poorly conceived definition!

Perhaps a better definition is "behavior that is consistent with the principles, norms, and standards of practice that have been agreed on by society."[31] But of course, to make this definition work, we would need to conduct surveys to keep abreast of the latest changes in public agreement. And surveys aren't particularly accurate. Look at how they missed the 2016 presidential election!

Successful business author John C. Maxwell pondered this definitional problem and concluded, "There's no such thing as *business* ethics."[32] There's just one set of rules for making good decisions, and those rules are the same for all situations, whether they be business related or not, or whether they be made yesterday, today, or tomorrow. In other words, ethics must be universal standards of right and wrong, not different standards for each entity in society. The Greek philosopher Aristotle pointed this

---

[31] Linda K. Trevino and Katherine A. Nelson, *Managing Business Ethics: Straight Talk About How to Do It Right* (New York: John Wiley and Sons, 1995), p. 14.

[32] John C. Maxwell (2003), *There's No Such Thing as "Business" Ethics: There's Only One Rule for Making Decisions* (New York: Time Warner Business Books, 2003), preface.

out many years ago: you can't have a peaceful society without a common understanding of what's right and wrong.[33]

The best definition yet would be this: "Ethics are well-founded standards of right and wrong that prescribe what humans ought to do, usually in terms of rights, obligations, benefits to society, fairness, or specific virtues."[34] The "well-founded" stipulation suggests that the individual ethical standards relate one to another without contradiction; and the focus suggests prescriptive behavior rather than observed behavior. "Well-founded" also suggests that there has been some agreement by society as to the veracity of the standards. So, when we discuss ethics in this book, we will be using this definition.

To sum up, we've reached a basic understanding that business can be "good" both qualitatively and quantitatively, and that good businesses strive to achieve both. We've also noted that business is a calling to service and it is not for everyone. Those who are motivated by love of money will have difficulty achieving business ends that are good both qualitatively *and* quantitatively. In addition, we've concluded that both business ethics and personal ethics should not be contradictory. Both consist of well-founded standards of behavior. Armed with these preliminary ideas, we can now move on to consider what some of these well-founded standards of behavior include. That's the subject of the next chapter.

---

[33] Aristotle, *Nicomachean Ethics*, trans. Terence Irwin, 2nd ed. (Indianapolis: Hackett, 1999), pp. 67–74.

[34] Manuel G. Velasquez, *Business Ethics Concepts and Cases*, 7th ed. (Upper Saddle River, NJ: Pearson, 2011), p. 10.

Questions for reflection

1. Think of a good company that you know something about. Is that company good because it achieves both quantitative and qualitative measures of success, and not just one or the other? What are the qualitative measures of success that come to mind?

2. What is the proper focus on profitability in a business? Can a business become so focused on profits that it loses its way? Or conversely, can a business become so focused on satisfying customers that it fails to survive? Do profits serve the common good?

3. Think about the reasons that influenced you to consider business as a career. How were you introduced to business? Who convinced you to explore this career? What is it about business that excites you? Do you feel a calling?

4. What do you believe is your purpose in life? As you go through life, how will you measure the accomplishment of this purpose?

5. Write a short list of the most important "well-founded standards of right and wrong."

Chapter 2

A Firm Foundation for Right and Wrong

The first principle of value that we need to rediscover is this: that all reality hinges on moral foundations. In other words, that this is a moral universe, and that there are moral laws of the universe just as abiding as the physical laws.

—Martin Luther King Jr., sermon, February 28, 1954

To make good decisions we need to understand the well-founded rules for conduct (or moral foundations) that comprise ethical reasoning. In this chapter, we'll look at the conclusions drawn by the Founding Fathers of the United States of America, who applied their natural law–based understanding to the question of ethics.

What is natural law?

One of my young friends rented a house, and he agreed, as part of the rental deal, to keep the lawn mowed. When the grass reached knee high, he figured he'd better try out the lawn mower he found in the back of the garage. After filling the tank with gasoline, he found that the engine wouldn't start. He examined the dip stick to check the oil level and found only a small glob of black goop at the bottom of the stick. Obviously, the crankcase was low on oil.

He looked around the garage for a can of oil, and, finding none, he considered whether he should drive to Wal-Mart to buy a quart. But then he started thinking. Why spend the money on oil, when all I need to do is to dilute the dried-up oil already in the crankcase? Let's see. Isn't gasoline a refined version of oil? Why not pour a little gasoline into the crankcase and see what happens? So he poured some gas into the crankcase, and after a few pulls on the starter rope, the engine came to life and he began to mow. You can imagine what happened next. Unfortunately, the engine soon began making some clanking noises, and a few minutes later it stopped completely.

What happened? The gasoline had acted as a solvent to clean the oil from the engine's internal components. Without lubrication, the engine bearings had overheated, and the engine was ruined.

If this student had downloaded a copy of the owner's manual provided by the manufacturer, he would have seen the warning written in 36-point boldface Helvetica type: "Do not put anything into the crankcase except motor oil that meets SAE specifications." This was just one of many rules, requirements, and safety warnings included in the manual, all intended to provide the user with guidance to maximize the useful life of the equipment.

Manufacturers routinely provide owner's manuals for their products. Good consumers pay attention to the guidelines, rules, and warnings contained in these manuals. Anytime there is a problem or question about the operation of the product, they refer to the owner's manual for advice. After all, the maker of the product knows how it works and therefore generally knows how the product is best used and maintained. This begs an important question: Did the Maker of the human race provide a guide for human interaction? Advocates of the natural law perspective suggest that the answer is yes. God did provide just such a manual.

How did natural law influence the founders of our country?

On July 4, 1776, the first Congress of the United States issued the "unanimous Declaration of the thirteen united States of America," and this became the founding document of our nation. The first sentence of this declaration refers to the "Laws of Nature and of Nature's God," and subsequent sentences establish that citizens have the right to change government when that government allows those natural laws to be violated. Obviously, the concept of natural law was deemed to be very important to the Founding Fathers, as it was used to justify the separation of the colonies from the British Empire and the subsequent establishment of a new and separate nation.

Just as a lawn-mower manufacturer builds certain capabilities and limitations into that device that necessitate rules of use, the founders of our nation believed that the Creator of the human race placed certain capabilities and limitations in our nature that require certain rules of conduct. When those rules are not followed, humans and society suffer adverse consequences. So, natural law consists of the insights of human conduct and behavior that our Creator has built into our nature.

Natural law is discernable through natural reason. When we follow the inclinations of the natural law, we align our lives according to the reason for our existence. Natural law is both

The Unanimous Declaration of the Thirteen United States of America

"When in the Course of human events it becomes necessary for one people to dissolve the political bands
which have connected them with another and to assume among the powers of the earth, the separate and
equal station to which the *Laws of Nature and of Nature's
God* entitle them, a decent respect to the opinions of
mankind requires that they should declare the causes
which impel them to the separation.

"We hold these truths to be self-evident, *that all men
are created equal*, that they are *endowed by their Creator
with certain unalienable Rights*, that among these are
Life, Liberty and the pursuit of Happiness.—That to
secure these rights, Governments are instituted among
Men, deriving their just powers from the consent of the
governed,—That whenever any Form of Government
becomes destructive of these ends, it is the Right of the
People to alter or to abolish it, and to institute a new
Government, laying its foundation on such principles
and organizing its powers in such form, as to them shall
seem most likely to effect their Safety and Happiness"
(emphasis added).

universal and immutable. Since this law is woven into our very
nature, the law commands and forbids with the same force everywhere and always. In essence, natural law is the "owner's manual" that prescribes rules of conduct for the human condition.

With this owner's manual, we should have assurance about what is right and wrong in our dealings with all those we meet. By following its precepts, we can do good while eliminating the bad from our lives. Through attentive knowledge of the natural law, we can avoid making stupid mistakes and damaging ourselves and those around us.

But where, you ask, can we pick up a copy of this owner's manual? Doctors at the hospital don't send a copy home with each new baby, do they?

Where do we find the natural law?

The idea of decent behavior seems to be obvious to everyone. The ancient Egyptians, Babylonians, Chinese, Greeks, and Romans all produced similar written codes detailing what is right and wrong. The human is gifted with a desire to seek and know truth, and life's evidence shows that when each of us takes the time to ponder the central questions about our existence, we find at least an outline of the answers lurking deep inside us. We come to realize that the universe must be governed by a God who knows what is best and orders all things accordingly. We conclude that we were created with in-built characteristics and designed to accomplish some purpose. And when we look at our natural behaviors, our intellect discovers universal moral truths involving fair play, decency, morality, and agreeable behavior that just seem to make good sense.

To be clear, the natural law is not instinct. Instincts provide automatic responses and do not require the use of reason. When the fast ball is sailing toward your head, your instinct informs you to duck quickly! But the natural law seems to work differently. It does not command an automatic response; rather, it causes us to contemplate, weigh alternatives, and decide before we undertake action.

Proponents of the natural law suggest that these laws are "written on our hearts," meaning that they correspond to our rightly ordered desires. Philosophers, poets, and saints have suggested that mankind generally desires to do good things and avoid evil. When we do good, we live well, but when we do evil, we do not live well. We have freedom always to follow or not follow the natural law, but this is akin to our freedom to smoke, binge drink, and stuff ourselves. We can do these things, but if we do them, there will be unhealthy consequences.

Historically, respect for the natural law has been a subject of concern for people of all religions. Christians and Jews believe that the Creator did not leave it for each of us to discern the law by ourselves. Rather, God reminded us by writing the essence of the natural law in "Ten Words" or "Commandments" on two stone tablets given to the prophet Moses on Mount Sinai.[35] Judeo-Christian tradition suggests that the first tablet contains guidelines that prescribe how we are to show love for our Creator. These include worship, use of images, appropriate speech, and setting aside one day each week devoted to our relationship with the Creator. The second tablet prescribes how we are to relate to one another in this world. These "second" commandments include guidelines regarding respect for authority, equitable treatment of others, chastity in speech and behavior, property ownership rights, truth, and self-control.

The first tablet's commands are distinctively Judeo-Christian. But you don't have to be a Jew or a Christian to appreciate the

---

[35] J. Budzisvewski, "The Second Tablet Project," *First Things* 124 (2002): 23–32.

second tablet's commands. There is a remarkable degree of agreement among the world's religions regarding these rules of interpersonal conduct. Every one of these commandments is supported in the teachings and writings reverenced by the major religions of the world.

For instance, the Quran, which Muslims believe is the word of God as revealed to Mohammed, contains similarly worded versions of each commandment. Buddhists advocate the "Ten Charges" and "Laws of Manu"; Hindus advocate the "Tenfold Law"; and Jainists advocate the "Ten Duties," all of which include ordinances generally consistent with the Bible's second-tablet commandments.

Even those who do not follow a particular faith usually acknowledge that these universal commandments provide wise and valuable counsel, the kind of advice that is considered common sense.[36] In addition, these second-tablet commands have had a profound influence on the development of law in many countries, especially the United States.

The second-tablet commands are these:

- *Honor your father and your mother.* This command engenders respect for all legitimate authority, beginning with one's parents, and forbids doing anything against, or failing to give honor and duty to, those in authority. Our laws regarding equity, regulatory compliance, pensions, and medical assistance for the elderly were all influenced by this commandment.
- *You shall not kill.* This implies that persons should undertake all lawful endeavors to preserve and protect their

---

[36] Robert Louis Wilken, "Keeping the Commandments," *First Things* 137 (2003): 33–38.

The Decalogue, or Ten Commandments
(Deuteronomy 5:6–21)

Tablet 1

1. I am the LORD your God, who brought you out of the land of Egypt, out of the house of bondage. You shall have no other gods before me. You shall not make for yourself a graven image, or any likeness of anything that is in heaven above, or that is on the earth beneath, or that is in the water under the earth; you shall not bow down to them or serve them; for I the LORD your God am a jealous God, visiting the iniquity of the fathers upon the children to the third and fourth generation of those who hate me, but showing steadfast love to thousands of those who love me and keep my commandments.

2. You shall not take the name of the LORD your God in vain: for the LORD will not hold him guiltless who takes his name in vain.

3. Observe the sabbath day, to keep it holy, as the LORD your God commanded you. Six days you shall labor, and do all your work; but the seventh day is a sabbath to the LORD your God; in it you shall not do any work, you, or your son, or your daughter, or your manservant, or your maidservant, or your ox, or your ass, or any of your cattle, or the sojourner who is within your gates,

that your manservant and your maidservant may rest as well as you. You shall remember that you were a servant in the land of Egypt, and the LORD your God brought you out thence with a mighty hand and an outstretched arm; therefore the LORD your God commanded you to keep the sabbath day.

Tablet 2

4. Honor your father and your mother, as the LORD your God commanded you; that your days may be prolonged, and that it may go well with you, in the land which the LORD your God gives you.
5. You shall not kill.
6. Neither shall you commit adultery.
7. Neither shall you steal.
8. Neither shall you bear false witness against your neighbor.
9. Neither shall you covet your neighbor's wife.
10. You shall not desire your neighbor's house, his field, or his manservant, or his maidservant, his ox, or his ass, or anything that is your neighbor's.

own lives and the lives of others, while forbidding the unjust taking of human life. Our laws regarding murder, manslaughter, suicide, assisted suicide, and abortion are all related to this commandment, as are laws relating to the care of the sick, the suffering, and the impoverished in our society.

• *You shall not commit adultery.* This commandment requires not only respect for the marriage bond but also the protection of chastity in speech and behavior. Our laws regarding pornography, indecency, and marriage are profoundly influenced by this commandment.

• *You shall not steal.* This commandment recognizes the property rights of individuals, and prohibits the taking of others' lawfully gained wealth. Our laws related to copyrights, patents, real and personal-property rights, and estates all reflect this commandment.

• *You shall not bear false witness against your neighbor.* This commandment requires maintaining and promoting truth among people, and enjoins anything that is injurious to someone's good name. Our laws relating to libel, slander, truth in advertising, and promotional communications reflect this commandment.

• *You shall not covet your neighbor's wife or your neighbor's goods.* These commands require self-control in dealings with others and prohibit scheming, fraud, and deceit to obtain what belongs to someone else. These commands are especially applicable to business. Our laws regarding fair competition are based upon controlling covetousness so that a level playing field is provided for free enterprise.

Taken together, the second-tablet commands provide an effective summary of the natural law. They provide overall guidelines for appropriate human conduct and promote respect for the equal dignity and worth of every human being. The commandments imply fair and equitable treatment for all.

The natural law has also been restated in other forms. Those who believe that the Decalogue is a little too religious might appreciate the following three rules proposed by Domènec Melé to summarize the natural law:

1. Good is to be done and pursued, and evil is to be avoided.
2. No human being should ever be treated as a means to an end. On the contrary, persons should be treated with respect and also with care and benevolence.
3. People, individuals, and social groups within a community should contribute to the common good of their community in accordance with the capabilities of each and should sacrifice individual interests when these conflict with the common good.[37]

Alternatively, one can summarize the natural law in one succinct statement, known as the Golden Rule: "Do unto others as you would have them do unto you."[38]

Does natural law apply to business?

The history of the human race demonstrates that humans frequently join together into groups, such as families, villages, social and charitable organizations, businesses, companies, states, and nations. Each of these organizations has a purpose, and each is formed because the group can be more effective or more efficient

---

[37] Domènec Melé, *Management Ethics: Placing Ethics at the Core of Good Management* (London: Palgrave MacMillan, 2012), pp. 28–32.

[38] See Matt. 22:36–40.

UNIAPAC and the Profit of Values

Why would thirty thousand business executives join together to learn how business can be structured to be more cooperative than competitive?

"What our organization is doing appeals to many business practitioners," explained Jose Maria Simone, president of UNIAPAC. "There's a strong desire on the part of many to promote an economy that is more respectful of mankind."

UNIAPAC is an international organization of business executives that promotes a vision of business called the "Profit of Values." Rather than focusing operations solely on financial goals, these executives look toward helping achieve societal and environmental values based on the intrinsic worth of the human person. The result is a better world in which to live.

According to UNIAPAC, business enterprises have a responsibility to all stakeholders of the business, which include shareholders and investors, persons who make

in accomplishing the purpose set forth than any individual can by acting alone. Organizations comprise individuals and are always agents of collective individual action. Accordingly, because natural law precepts apply to individuals, they apply to organizations by extension. That is why our nation's founders were so upset with the British government. When measured against the natural law, the British government was "stealing" the personal up the enterprise and their families, suppliers, distributors, clients, consumers, governments, the community, competitors, and future generations. This responsibility requires:

- respect for the dignity of human persons and the promotion of their comprehensive development
- promotion of the common good, with peace, stability, and the security of a just order
- management according to subsidiarity so that workers can develop to their full potential
- a determination to express solidarity with all, especially the disadvantaged and the weak

UNIAPAC was established in 1931 among Belgian, French, and Dutch businessmen. It was expanded in 1949 to include executives in other European countries. Today its official English-language name is "International Christian Union of Business Executives," and it has members in twenty-three countries.*

*More information is available at www.uniapac.org.

property of the citizens in the thirteen colonies through its practice of "taxation without representation."

All organizations, no matter what their purpose, should observe the natural law. A firm that deceives its investors and customers, or falsifies information provided to government agencies, or produces unsafe products that could harm those who use them, violates the natural law.

Leaders of these organizations have the same obligation that our Founding Fathers had. Any violations of the natural law should be identified and corrected immediately. If the organization somehow persists in the violation, the leader should declare his or her independence from that organization and move to another one that respects the commands of the natural law.

What are the objections to natural law?

Not everyone is a fan of natural law theory. Objections arise in at least two areas. First, some detractors suggest that we seem to find more disagreement about morality than we would expect if universal moral principles were discernable by all.[39] Second, atheists are bothered that natural law theory implies that there exists a deity that began the universe and exercises continuing dominion over all creation. In the following paragraphs, we'll look at each objection.

First, why do people disagree regarding morality? Even though there is broad agreement on the commandments themselves, there is often disagreement regarding their application in different contexts. These varied interpretations are the principal reason we see differences in the rights and obligations of citizens of different nations, and disagreements as to what the right course of action might be in specific situations. The rules are certainly clear at the top level — obey authority, protect life, observe chastity, respect private property, be honest, and moderate your desires — and natural law advocates are in agreement with these principles. But ethical decisions are by their nature difficult, and disagreements invariably occur at the operational level where

---

[39] McCarthy, *Catholic Social Teaching*, p. 117.

many factors influence human behavior and individual biases affect ethical judgments.

Some like to be pragmatic and resist rigid characterizations of right and wrong. Is it okay to stretch the truth and answer someone's "How's it going?" with "Great!" even though you're having a rough day? Or, is it okay to "borrow" a paperclip from the office to organize something for use at home? Some argue that any lying and stealing is morally wrong; others suggest that when there's no harm, there's no foul, and many minor violations of the natural law should be deemed harmless.

Disagreements occur when trying to resolve situations in which two commandments are involved. For instance, one person steals, another murders. Is it appropriate for society to apply the same jail term to both offenders?

Some commandments would seem to be more important than others. In Jesus' time, people were wondering which commands were the more important ones and which were less important. By knowing how they ranked, people would be more readily able to come to an agreement when dealing with ethical dilemmas. A lawyer even asked Jesus to name the greatest of the commandments. Presumably, he planned to continue his line of questioning with "What's the next greatest commandment, and the next?" until he had Jesus rank-order all ten.

However, Jesus answered in a way that put a stop to further inquiry. His reply was, "You shall love the Lord your God with all your heart, with all your soul and with all your mind. This is the great and first commandment. And a second is like it. You shall love your neighbor as yourself. On these two commandments depend all the law and the prophets" (Matt. 22:36–40).

In effect, Jesus told the lawyer that there was unity between the first-tablet commands (how we go about loving God) and the second-tablet commands (how we go about loving each other). Thus, Christian tradition holds that the first group of commands is fundamental in establishing a right relationship with our neighbor. Christianity teaches that when you love God, you will receive the encouragement and fortitude necessary to love your neighbor as yourself. In so doing, you are given the power to obey the second-tablet commands.

The second objection relates to whether it is necessary to believe in God to accept natural law. This is an important question. While some believe that integrating faith with reason provides a more fruitful means to know how things work, pure scientists want to restrict analysis to what we can observe. Since God is not discernable through our senses, many scientists do not value any theory that involves the presence of God as Creator, or First Mover.

Religion performs an important function in that it helps inform individual consciences as to the interpretation and application of the natural law. The practice of faith leads to a systematic understanding that becomes second nature and helps individuals become more effective in making good decisions regarding the ethical dilemmas they face.

Yes, you are correct. World religions do hold differing perspectives about the nature of the Creator and what we should do to maintain a right relationship. But, despite this diversity, people of faith generally agree that the second-tablet commandments provide a summary of the necessary guidelines for good human behavior. Unfortunately, this rationale doesn't help the atheist.

Aristotle was the first to develop natural law theory, and he wasn't particularly religious. But later, Thomas Aquinas built upon Aristotle's foundation and his involvement gave the theory a close Christian connection. The belief that humans are not random products of unguided evolution, but that an intelligent Being created us in a certain way, provides a powerful, compelling rationale for belief in the natural law as a meaningful system.

If one believes that our nature is simply the result of happenstance, however, he has little incentive to accept the relationships we observe in human interaction as having moral force. One could still accept these relationships as appropriate guides of conduct, but the lack of connection to a supreme authority reduces their importance.

Natural law presumes that by means of our nature God calls us to respond in a certain way, and no amount of training, personal development, or watching old reruns of *The Andy Griffith Show* will cause us to change our nature. Consequently, honesty in human interaction was just as important ten thousand years ago as it is today and will be ten thousand years in the future. This consistency poses a philosophical problem for those who believe in evolution, and in the idea that the human race changes, or naturally selects, due to environmental factors. If human nature changes through evolution, then natural law must change as well, or so they argue. What was written three millennia ago can't still be valid today, can it?

There a similar overarching concern that I've heard from both students and businesspeople, and it goes like this: "Everywhere we look, we see that society has made great progress in reducing poverty, curing illness, and improving the way people live. Haven't there been similar advancements in the way we understand ethics? Natural law theory is ancient — certainly there must be something better."

Is there something better? Is there an approach for understanding right and wrong that can satisfy atheists and gain universal agreement? Over the years, philosophers have tried to devise an approach to ethics that can effectively replace the natural law. In the next chapter, we'll review their best efforts.

Questions for reflection

1. Is "natural law" the appropriate name to describe the idea that humans respond consistently to the way others treat them, and respond best when treatment corresponds to certain rules of conduct?

2. Write a list of rules of personal conduct that would engender trust in your coworkers. Do the second-tablet commands capture everything on your list? Is there anything missing?

3. Look at the list you wrote for question 2 and select what you consider to be the most important rule, the one that might cause the most harm when violated. Provide a solid rationale for your selection.

4. Consider whether religious faith affects how one determines ethical behavior. What can you say to convince someone with no religious faith to support the second-tablet commandments as appropriate rules of behavior?

Chapter 3

Finding Clarity in the Big Picture

*Wise men speak because they have something to
say; fools because they have to say something.*

—Attributed to Plato

*Think left and think right and think low and think high.
Oh, the thinks you can think up if only you try!*

—Dr. Seuss, *Oh, the Thinks You Can Think*

Some of the world's brightest minds have devoted their talents to
understanding ethics and developing guidance for good decision-
making. Like the forest ranger who erects a lookout tower, these
philosophers have taken a "big picture" view of ethical decision-
making. A review of these contributions together with their
limitations is instructive for anyone interested in understanding
business ethics. Following are discussions of five of the more well-
known theories that have gained followers through the years.

What are the key competing theories of ethics?

The five most significant theories of ethics are ethical egoism,
moral relativism, utilitarianism, duty ethics, and virtue ethics.

Ethical egoism is the simple idea that individuals should act in their own self-interest when making moral decisions. Egoism claims that the best moral choice is the one that maximizes benefits to self, whether in the short or long term. The interests of others are not given any consideration in the analysis.

James Rachels, one of ethical egoism's leading proponents, provided the following two-part defense for this moral philosophy. First,

> Each of us is intimately familiar with our own individual wants and needs. Moreover, each of us is uniquely placed to pursue those wants and needs effectively. At the same time, we know the desires and needs of others only imperfectly, and we are not well situated to pursue them. Therefore, it is reasonable to believe that if we set out to be "our brother's keeper," we would often bungle the job and end up doing more mischief than good.[40]

Second, competing ethical approaches undervalue an individual's real worth and are therefore destructive to society. Philosopher Ayn Rand wrote that, "if a man accepts the ethics of altruism, his first concern is not how to live his life but how to sacrifice it." This doesn't make much sense because "the purpose of morality is to teach you not to suffer and die, but to enjoy yourself and live."[41]

---

[40] James Rachels, "Ethical Egoism," in *Reason and Responsibility: Readings in Some Basic Problems of Philosophy*, ed. Joel Feinberg and Russ Shafer-Landau (Belmont, CA: Thomson Wadsworth, 2008), pp. 532–540.

[41] Ayn Rand, "Faith and Force, the Destroyers of the Modern World: The Age of Guilt," *Vital Speeches of the Day* 26, no. 20 (August 1960): 630–636.

So, Rachels is saying that egoism is good because we can't know what our neighbor truly needs and any other approach devalues the individual.

Christianity provides an effective rejoinder to both defenses. Scripture challenges us to assume our Christian obligations of clothing the poor, feeding the hungry, ministering to the sick, and visiting the incarcerated. Even though we are not very good at it, Scripture clearly indicates that we *are* our brothers' keepers, and we seem to have the ability and mandate to improve our effectiveness in undertaking this obligation. Jesus Christ, through His life, death, and Resurrection, demonstrated a selfless love for others. His command to "love one another as I have loved you" (John 15:12) identifies the path to true joy in this life and the next. How can one be Christian and be an ethical egoist at the same time?

Other criticisms of ethical egoism include (1) the claim that egoists misrepresent the true nature of altruism by arguing that it is the only alternative; and (2) egoists are conflicted regarding the adoption of ethical egoism by others because the more egoists there are, the more difficult it will be for an egoist to maximize his or her own self-interest. My principal concern is the one raised by Kurt Baier: that ethical egoism provides no moral basis for the resolution of conflicts of interest and, all too often, actually spawns them.[42] Ethical egoism divides people into two types—self and other—and discriminates against one type on the basis of some arbitrary disparity. To me this sounds a great deal like bigotry.

---

[42] John Hospers, "Baier and Medlin on Ethical Egoism," *Philosophical Studies* 12, nos. 1–2 (January–February 1961): 10–16.

Despite the criticisms, despite the lack of contemporary advocates, and despite the fact that "egoism" is a term that is no longer "politically correct," many people still act as if they were adhering to this philosophy. Sadly, I've run into this type of individual many times in business situations.

Moral relativism is the idea that all points of view are equally valid, and that all truth is relative. Relativism owes its initial development to the Greek philosopher Protagoras, who famously proclaimed, "Man is the measure of all things."[43] His theory proposed that all ethical judgments differ according to circumstances, persons, and cultural phenomena. Accordingly, what one sees and hears can be only subjectively true, that is, true to the observer; it can never be objectively true, or true when measured against some universal moral standard.

Under relativism, if one statement is judged to be true for one group, and an opposite statement is judged to be true for a second group, these two opposite statements may both be "correct." (I've had students try to argue for better test grades based on this philosophy of relativism, but with little success. They point out that the answer they provided was true to them and deserves full credit; but I point out that the answer is not true to me, and I'm the one who assigns the grade!)

Relativism presumes that everything depends on the viewpoint of the beholder. The relativist conforms to his own moral standard by deciding what he believes is right, and consequently, he cannot be challenged that he is wrong.

For example, suppose Sandra believes that misstating the financial condition of the company is acceptable since it might

---

[43] William K. C. Guthrie, *The Sophists* (New York: Cambridge University Press, 1877), pp. 262–263.

assist the firm in obtaining a lucrative contract. This would be considered an ethical choice for Sandra. Conversely, if Sally believes such misstating is wrong, then it would be unethical for Sally to do it. Thus, relativism isn't particularly helpful as a decision-making tool. No matter what we decide, we can generally find someone who says that it is ethical.

Accordingly, a common argument against relativism is that it inherently contradicts itself.[44] Relativism rules out absolutes. Yet consider the statement "All is relative." Although it summarizes relativism, it is an absolute statement that presupposes that not all truths are relative!

Another problem is that if there is no truth beyond one group's belief that something is true, then that group cannot adequately test or modify its own beliefs or recognize when those beliefs are false or mistaken. Relativizing truth destroys the distinction between truth and belief.

The Catholic Church regards the spread of relativism as one of the most significant problems for faith and morals today. Because relativism is a denial of absolute truth, it leads to the denial of both the possibility of sin and the reality of God. The result is a failure to listen to the gospel. Pope Benedict XVI lamented:

> Today, a particularly insidious obstacle to the task of education is the massive presence in our society and culture of that relativism which, recognizing nothing as definitive, leaves as the ultimate criterion only the self with its desires. And under the semblance of freedom it becomes

---

[44] Keith Dixon, "Is Cultural Relativism Self-Refuting?" *British Journal of Sociology* 28, no. 1 (March 1977).

a prison for each one, for it separates people from one another, locking each person into his or her own ego.[45]

Relativism holds that it's okay for me to believe what I want and it's okay for you to believe what you want, and therefore we don't need to discuss our differences. This approach reduces our opportunities to learn from one another. And it certainly doesn't provide good guidance as to what is ethical in any situation.

Utilitarianism, also referred to as the "greatest happiness principle," is the idea that the best moral action is the one that maximizes utility, where utility is defined as pleasure minus pain. Unlike egoism, in which only the individual is considered in the decision, utilitarianism treats everyone affected as having equal interests. The ethical decision is the one that maximizes the pleasure and minimizes the pain for everyone affected by the action.

The first proponent of utilitarianism was the English philosopher Jeremy Bentham, who proposed a quantitative method for calculating the net value of pleasure minus pain, and this formula became known as the "hedonic calculus." The formula required that the value of pleasure and pain be measured according to its intensity, duration, and likelihood, together with the number of people affected.[46] In essence, the formula was an early attempt at developing a cost-benefit analysis.

In a notorious application of utilitarianism in the 1970s, Ford Motor Company attempted to decide whether it made ethical

---

[45] Benedict XVI, Address to participants in the Ecclesial Diocesan Convention of Rome, June 6, 2005.

[46] Jeremy Bentham, *The Principles of Morals and Legislation* (1789).

sense to add a gas-tank shield to one of its vehicles. The car was the Pinto, an inexpensive vehicle designed to compete with the VW Beetle and the Toyota Corolla in the U.S. market.

The Pinto gas tank was designed to fit between the rear axle and the rear bumper, and crash tests indicated that in a rear-end collision, the tank might get crushed against the rear axle and explode, engulfing the car in flames. The value of pleasure in this case was calculated based on an estimate of how much less consumers would have to pay for the car if the costs of installing the shield did not have to be incurred. The value of pain was calculated based on estimated doctor and hospitalization costs of treating burn injuries together with actuarial tables that valued the costs of fatalities.[47]

In this case, the calculations showed that the aggregate "pleasure" of buying a car for less money outweighed the "pain" or estimated costs of loss of life and limb, so building cars without a gas-tank shield was deemed to be the ethical choice. But had the company used a higher value for the "cost" of burn injuries, the calculation may well have gone the other way. Many regard this incident as a cost-benefit analysis gone wrong.

Bentham's leading advocate, John Stuart Mill, rejected a purely quantitative measurement for utilitarianism and proposed a more qualitative approach.[48] Consequently, today's utilitarian rarely pulls out the calculator for detailed analysis, but rather weighs both pleasure and pain in more qualitative terms. Had Mill worked for Ford Motor Company at the time of the Pinto

---

[47] William Shaw and Vincent Barry, *Moral Issues in Business*, 8th ed. (Belmont, CA: Wadsworth, 2001), pp. 83–86.

[48] John Stuart Mill, *Utilitarianism*, ed. Roger Crisp (Oxford: Oxford University Press, 1998), p. 56.

incident, he may very well have suggested that burn pain intensity is qualitatively much greater and counts more than any pleasure resulting from a lower price. If that were the case, the shield installation would be the better ethical choice.

Critics have voiced two concerns about utilitarianism. First, the determination of pleasure and pain is often difficult and impractical. Some people take pleasure in shopping to find a deal, others love playing golf, and still others view shopping or playing golf to be painful! Neither pleasure nor pain is the same among people with varying interests and concerns, and thus the idea of aggregating utility presents significant problems. For instance, how does one value human life? Is the value of a Super Bowl MVP who earns $20 million per year the same as the value of a young child with no apparent skills and an unknown future? These value determinations are complex, difficult, and time-consuming.

Second, the utility-decision criterion ignores social justice[49] and promotes a major-minority imbalance. Suppose the action being evaluated causes pleasure for all brown-eyed people but causes pain for all blue-eyed people. If the majority of people have brown eyes, then utilitarianism will favor the action because it will cause more pleasure than pain. This is a ridiculous example, of course, but I think you get the point. Because of these deficiencies, utilitarianism is a defective approach.

Duty ethics (or deontology) is a moral philosophy that looks for the best set of rules to live by to fulfill one's duty.[50] This ap-

---

[49] H. J. McCloskey, "An Examination of Restricted Utilitarianism," *Philosophical Review* 66, no. 4 (October 1957): 466–485.

[50] Shelby Hunt and Scott Vitell, "A General Theory of Marketing Ethics," *Journal of Macromarketing* 6 (Spring 1986): 5–16.

proach was created by German philosopher Immanuel Kant to oppose utilitarianism, a theory he found distasteful.[51]

The key idea in Kant's formulation is the categorical imperative, which determines moral principles through the question of duty and a logical test of consistency. Two questions can be used to understand whether the action is an imperative: First, can I rationally will that everyone act as I propose to act, making this a universal rule? And second, does my action respect the goals of human beings rather than merely using people for my own purposes? If the answer to both questions is yes, the action is considered a categorical imperative and is considered moral.

Let's take an example. Suppose a convenience store has an ice machine that has been leaking, creating a puddle of water on the floor. Does duty ethics require that the owner of the convenience store repair the ice machine and remove the puddle?

Applying the first logical test of consistency, the answer is yes, it does make sense to require the owner of a broken ice machine to repair or replace the malfunctioning equipment before someone slips and gets hurt. A universal rule requiring owners to eliminate safety hazards in their stores is certainly rational. Applying the second question, the answer is also yes: eliminating the hazard respects the goals of people who might visit the store and does not treat them as means to an end. Accordingly, the store owner has a categorical imperative to eliminate the hazard.

Kant's approach is interesting and laudable, but there are some serious deficiencies. The most serious is that Kant minimizes the moral significance of the action itself and rests the decision on the intention of the actor. Since acts can have intentions

---

[51] Immanuel Kant, *Foundations of the Metaphysics of Morals* (New York: Macmillan, 1969).

of their own that differ from the intentions of the actors, we can end up determining that doing something shady, such as falsifying records to hire illegals at low wages, is morally correct. Why? Because doing so provides employment for those who need it. In other words, duty ethics would seem to allow the ends (providing employment) to justify the means (falsifying records).

Another deficiency is that duty ethics does not recognize the moral worthiness of actions motivated purely by generosity or charity, when no element of conforming to duty is present. Consequently, a businesswoman who volunteers her time to work in a soup kitchen would be committing an immoral act. While offering great promise, duty ethics fall short of its goal.

Virtue ethics is the moral philosophy that emphasizes the role of good character in ethical decision-making. This philosophy takes its inspiration from Plato[52] and Aristotle,[53] who reasoned that happiness is the ultimate goal of human existence and that the best way to be happy is to develop behavioral habits directed toward achieving good results. When a person is oriented toward the good, and develops skills to achieve that good, that individual will naturally be happy. Both Greek thinkers concluded that the virtues of prudence, justice, courage, and moderation were the most important virtues, and individuals who developed proficiency in these four would naturally become good ethical decision-makers.

Virtue ethics places emphasis on being rather than on doing, and on developing character rather than on analyzing ethicality.

---

[52] Darren J. Sheppard, *Plato's Republic* (Bloomington, IN: Indiana University Press, 1969).

[53] David Bostock, *Aristotle's Ethics* (New York: Oxford University Press, 2000).

Because actions naturally flow from character, a just person will tend to do just acts, a prudent person will tend to do prudent acts, and a person who is both just and prudent will tend to do both. When an individual develops a virtuous character, then ethical decision-making follows easily.

But there is one minor limitation. Getting everyone to agree on which virtues are the most important for decision-making seems to be difficult. Even Aristotle and Plato disagreed once they got past the first four, and Thomas Aquinas added three more to the most important list—faith, hope, and charity.[54]

Agreeing on one list is important for decision-making. If one business person favors the virtue of magnanimity and another favors the virtue of cleanliness, then the two may not agree on the proper ethical course of action in an employment situation. Each would gravitate toward different criteria for judgment. One might favor hiring the magnanimous candidate, while the other might favor the clean candidate.

How can we decide which is the best approach?

The basic differences among these philosophies can be amplified by examining the level of goal setting employed in their execution. There are four levels of goals: (1) personal goals, (2) group goals, (3) societal goals, and (4) transcendent goals. These are summarized in the accompanying chart (see next page).

---

[54] Christopher Kaczor, *Thomas Aquinas on Faith, Hope, and Love: Edited and Explained for Everyone* (Ave Maria, FL: Sapientia Press, 2008).

Force for Good

Four Levels of Goal Setting

Level 1: "Do What's Good for Me"

Objectives	Maximize pleasure and minimize pain; gain advantage over others.
Characteristics	Obligation is to self alone. No desire for common, intrinsic, or ultimate good. Gratification is immediate. Negatives are lack of self-worth, fear of tangible loss/harm, boredom, jealousy, isolation, and cynicism.
Conceptual Foundation:	Modern egoism

Level 2: "Do What's Good for My Group"

Objectives	Integral part of successful group; gain advantage over other groups.
Characteristics	Promotion of group is primary; personal power and control are key. Gratification is short-term. Negatives are fear of failure and uncontrolled competitiveness.
Conceptual Foundation:	Relativism

Level 3: "Do What's Good for the Majority"

Objectives	Do good beyond self.
Characteristics	Principles include justice, love, and community. Intrinsic goodness is an end in itself. Decisions are focused on the greater good. Gratification tends to be longer-term.
Conceptual Foundation:	Utilitarianism

Level 4: "Do What's Best for Everyone"	
Objectives	Participate in giving and receiving ultimate meaning, goodness, ideals, and love.
Characteristics	Good is an ultimate. Principles include ultimate truth, love, justice, and beauty. Gratification is eternal.
Conceptual Foundation:	Natural law theory and virtue ethics

At the first level, the individual strives to maximize self-interest by doing "what's good for me." Modern egoism is a philosophy based at this first level, and insights from this philosophy might very well be beneficial if the goal is to win at a game of cards or another game involving individual players. But it has limited applicability if the goal is to run a complex business.

At the second level, the goal is for "my team" to win, and philosophies directed at this level, such as relativism, might provide the business leader with insights on how to select what's beneficial for the team. This level of goal setting might make sense if the object was to win the Olympic Gold Medal in hockey, for instance, but it is not very applicable for leaders of a business organization when that organization has expectations to deliver benefits to customers, suppliers, municipalities, and those other than team members.

At the third level, the goal is to do good beyond self, so that others benefit. The basic decision rule is to do what's best for the majority — if more people profit from the action than those who lose, then the action is considered moral. Utilitarianism may provide insights into decision-making if you are a politician in a representative democracy, or a business executive attempting to discern moral action when competing stakeholder groups do not benefit equally. Certainly, this level of goal setting is superior to the first two levels.

At the fourth level, the goal is to make decisions that correspond to giving and receiving ultimate truth, meaning, goodness, and love. In that way, decision-making respects what is best not just for one individual, one group, or the majority of people but for everyone. The natural law, duty ethics, and virtue ethics operate at this fourth level. For the founders of our country and, indeed, for most Americans today, ultimate truth and meaning was defined, and continues to be defined, by our Creator. Consequently, when we do what God wants us to do, we benefit in His creation to the maximum extent. When we engage at this level of goal setting, good becomes an ultimate and gratification tends to become eternal.

Contrary to what we see in the news media, decision-making should not revolve around conflict between the "rights" of one group and the "rights" of another. Spirited conflict makes news and sells newspapers and helps inform politicians about which issues in society need attention. Polling data can serve the purpose of helping assess what specific groups of people believe should be done. Business organization decision-making, however, is not about pitting one group against another; that's goal setting at the second level. Nor is it about polling the population to see which action they favor; that's goal setting at the third level.

Good ethical decision-making in business situations is done at the fourth level, where the objective is to make balanced decisions that benefit everyone, not just for now, but in the future as well.

Let's apply these levels to an example. When a technology company prices its products, it could set the price schedule so that:

- current quarter profitability is maximized, thereby increasing the CEO's quarterly bonus compensation (level 1)
- shareholder dividends are maximized (level 2)
- shareholders and consumers are both happy (level 3)
- all stakeholders are satisfied and poor consumers with little discretionary income can participate by buying the product (level 4)

Since the level 4 alternative promises to benefit the common good, it is likely the preferred option.

What's the bottom line on alternatives to natural law?

Our discussion of ethics in chapter 2 concluded that natural law theory provided the well-founded rules for conduct that are needed to guide ethical behavior. But we also recognized that there are competing approaches, and before we pinned our hopes on one approach, we wanted to evaluate the alternatives.

So, here in chapter 3, we have examined modern egoism, ethical relativism, utilitarianism, duty ethics, and virtue ethics, and what do you think? Do any of them provide a better approach than natural law theory? Virtue ethics and duty ethics provide some interesting insights, but egoism, relativism, and utilitarianism have inherent problems that make them intellectually deficient. Paraphrasing Dr. Seuss, it would appear that we've thought lots of "thinks," but none of them is better than where we started. Efforts to create a moral philosophy that is superior to natural law have come up empty.

Consequently, our discussion reaffirms that natural law theory reflected in the fundamental expression of laws for a society steeped in the Judeo-Christian tradition—the Ten Commandments, or Decalogue—is an ideal basis for ethical decision-making. When organizations strive to follow the rules presented in the second tablet, they are automatically drawn to decision-making at the fourth level.

But what about the concern that natural law is "old hat"? Hasn't there been further development in natural law theory to make it fresh and applicable to current issues? And hasn't anyone looked at incorporating virtue ethics within natural law theory?

What is the integrity-based perspective?

Integrity is the idea that any one component of something is consistent with every other component. A person with integrity responds appropriately when confronted with an ethical issue—not just once, but every time. A business with integrity consistently follows moral principles in all areas of its operation. No matter where you look in that business—marketing, sales, service, manufacturing, accounting, or finance—the overriding moral compass is complete and functioning effectively.

You see, if your firm is ethical in one area, but not in all areas, yours is not an ethical organization. If your firm is ethical 98 percent of the time, but you ignore the other 2 percent because "nobody's perfect," yours is not an ethical organization.

Think about this statement. It is easier to follow a rule 100 percent of the time than it is to allow occasional exceptions. When occasional exceptions are allowed, then the line of demarcation between right and wrong suddenly becomes very difficult to draw. "Gee, we made that exception last time and nothing happened. We may as well do it again." Soon, the standard becomes an unreachable ideal rather than an expectation, and the whole organization becomes lax.

But there is more to the integrity approach to ethics than consistency. Integrity begins with the natural law, incorporates some key business virtues, and adds important principles contained in the body of knowledge known as Catholic Social Doctrine (CSD; see accompanying diagram), the definitive papal interpretation of faith and reason as applied to human interaction. CSD is the result of the best thinking by saints and scholars who have analyzed the human condition through the centuries. While it reflects universal and time-tested truths, it is also fresh, contemporary, and supported by empirical research. Integrity requires that everyone in the organization follow the same principles of ethical decision-making. In this way, doing the right thing is integrated throughout the organization.

CSD reflects the fact that the Catholic Church has frequently sought to provide guidance on various topics of interest by issuing encyclical letters. These documents are intended for broad distribution and directed to people of all faiths. They represent

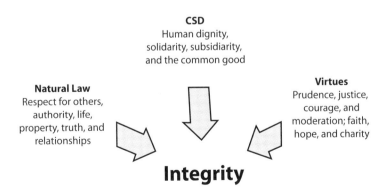

CSD
Human dignity,
solidarity, subsidiarity,
and the common good

Natural Law
Respect for others,
authority, life,
property, truth, and
relationships

Virtues
Prudence, justice,
courage, and
moderation; faith,
hope, and charity

Integrity

the Church's best thinking about how people should respond to social issues, yet the advice presented is consistent with the gospel message.

Encyclicals are major teaching documents issued under papal authority and represent moral teaching and guidance that incorporate the work of the best theologians, philosophers, and scientists. On the Vatican website, you'll find numerous encyclicals, many of which deal with social issues.

CSD builds upon the natural law and virtue ethics. It is unfortunate that many people, including many Catholics, do not know and understand the key teachings of CSD. It is called the Church's "best kept secret," not because the Church has attempted to keep this work hidden, but because Catholics in the pews generally learn their Faith through Sunday preaching, rather than by reading papal writings.

Yet, when Bible-inspired Christians are exposed to the principles of CSD, they tend to respond favorably because they see the scriptural connections to each of the principles. I've listed some of those connections in the accompanying chart.

The doctrine consists of four major principles that provide overall direction and focus: (1) human dignity, (2) solidarity, (3) subsidiarity, and (4) the common good. Let's briefly summarize each one, and describe their implications in the practice of business.

Human dignity is the "people first" principle. It recognizes that men and women are uniquely created in the image and likeness of God and thus have transcendent dignity. This dignity requires that the well-being of the individual person is the first priority in everything that we do. Productive work should be organized so that it employs individuals in meaningful occupations, creates products that have real value, and develops the worker's body, mind, and spirit. Pope John XXIII taught that if the whole structure and organization of an economic system is such as to compromise human dignity, to lessen a man's sense of responsibility or rob him of opportunity for exercising personal initiative, then such a system is altogether unjust — no matter how much wealth it produces, or how justly or equitably such wealth is distributed.

Solidarity is the "teamwork" principle; it reflects the inherent social nature of the human person and recognizes that only within relationships with others through family, work, and community do we fully develop our individual potential. We are created to work with those around us, and, like any good team player, we have an obligation to assist other members of the team to improve their game so that the team does well. This means lending a hand to any individual in need or in trouble. Because every human being is a team member on "Team Earth," firms have an obligation to help those within their reach who have special needs or who may be underserved for any reason.

Subsidiarity is the "personal responsibility" principle and is rooted in the conviction that the full development of human beings requires complete use of individual capability, intelligence, and initiative. But this principle applies to all entities in society, including the family, church, community, state, and nation. Each entity has an area of responsibility, some small and some large, in which they are in control. Others entities should not interfere with that control unless the first entity invites assistance. Pope Benedict remarked that a

> society that honors the principle of subsidiarity liberates people from a sense of despondency and hopelessness, granting them the freedom to engage with one another in the spheres of commerce, politics, and culture. When those

Scriptural Support for the Core
Principles of Catholic Social Doctrine

All four principles can be viewed as providing substance to Jesus' command to "love one another as I have loved you" (John 13:34–35; 15:12–13; cf. Matt. 22:37-39). We express this love by elevating these principles in our relationships with others.

- *Human dignity*. Genesis describes how humans were created in the image and likeness of God (1:26–31). No other creatures were made with this special dignity accorded to men and women. Further, the stories of the Good Samaritan (Luke 10:25–37) and the Samaritan woman (John 4:1–42) reinforce the importance of the individual person as having special dignity.
- *Solidarity*. St. Paul's description of the Church as one Body reminds us, in a broader context, that everyone is indispensable, even the weaker members of society. If one person suffers, then everyone suffers together; if one person is honored, then all rejoice together (1 Cor. 12:12–26). Scripture also encourages us to love others (Rom. 13:8–10), to seek the good for others (Ps. 122), and even to lay down our lives for others (1 John 3:16–18).
- *Subsidiarity*. A number of scriptural passages advocate personal responsibility, including the

advice to make friends with your accuser on the
way to court (Matt. 5:25) and to provide for
family and relatives (1 Tim. 5:8) and St. Paul's
comments criticizing idleness and unwillingness
to work (2 Thess. 3:10).

* *Common good.* The Parable of the Talents (Matt.
25:14–30) encourages us all to use the gifts God
has given us to help make the world a better
place; this idea is reinforced in 1 Peter 4:10; 2
Corinthians 9:6–7; John 3:27; and 1 Timothy
6:17–19.

responsible for the public good attune themselves to the
natural human desire for self-governance based upon subsidiarity, they leave space for individual responsibility and
initiative, but most importantly, they leave space for love.

The principle of subsidiarity is superior to what we usually mean
by delegation. One who delegates confers power temporarily but
can take it back at any time. With subsidiarity, the power resides
permanently with the lower entity. It can't be taken back. When
subsidiarity is implemented correctly, employees who are trusted
and trained know precisely the extent of their responsibilities and
are free to make good decisions. Consequently, they are free to
develop as co-entrepreneurs in the business in which they work.

The *common good* is the "human flourishing" principle, as it
promotes conditions in which all individuals and groups reach
their fulfillment more fully and more easily.

We're not talking about a utilitarian-style summation where we add together the achievement level of each individual and then arrive at a total. Rather, the common-good principle represents what everyone holds in common: it's the community dimension of the moral good.

A society that has the common good in mind organizes so that it can be at the service of individual persons at every level of development. For businesses, the principle of the common good requires producing truly good goods and services that meet authentic human needs while uplifting mind, body, and spirit. Deep River Snacks attempts to do this in their marketing efforts. (See "Implementing Integrity at Deep River Snacks.")

You've probably noticed that there is some slight tension among all four principles, especially between human dignity and the common good, and also between subsidiarity and

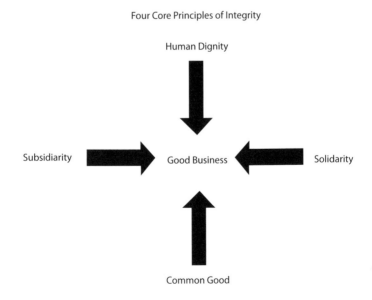

Four Core Principles of Integrity

Human Dignity

Subsidiarity   Good Business   Solidarity

Common Good

Implementing Integrity at Deep River Snacks

Deep River Snacks is about more than just a bag of chips. According to its president and founder, James Goldberg, this is a company that is committed to "doing right in everything they do."

"We operate the first LEED platinum snack food manufacturing plant in the world," James boasts on the Deep River website. "Where possible, we also incorporate sustainable materials in packaging and distribution, and use non-GMO potatoes, corn, and sunflower oil. We're all natural, gluten-free, and kosher."

But there's another aspect of the brand's promotion that excites many customers. Each package label features a special charity partner that has touched the life of a Deep River Snacks employee. James Goldberg explains, "We think it's important to raise awareness for these causes, and we hope customers will take a few moments to learn more about these special charitable organizations. We are committed to donating at least 10 percent of net profits to these, and to other charities, each year."

Here's an example taken from a product label:

We enthusiastically support various non-profit organizations by highlighting a different charity on every flavor of Deep River Snacks. If this charity resonates with you, please consider helping its cause! Deep River Snacks supports the

> Leukemia & Lymphoma Society because I am a stage 4 Non-Hodgkin's Lymphoma survivor and my wish is to raise awareness and to give support to those affected by this disease. For this reason, please consider supporting the LLS to "leave a legacy of hope." —Lee Whiting/VP of Sales

solidarity. Integrity requires balance between these two pairs. Sure, we always put people first, but we do so in a way that looks toward the lasting legacy that our actions take on society. And, while we always support our team members, we do so in a way that doesn't undermine their individual responsibility and authority.

Before we go any further, I'd like to acknowledge the pushback that I often get when I begin to talk about these CSD principles of integrity. Typically, it goes something like this: "Hold on here. I'm not interested in idealistic principles! I want something pragmatic that really works in real-life situations. I'm running a business here, not a church. Please give me the practical version!"

I want to assure you that all four of the integrity principles are highly pragmatic. They are based on the nature of man and tested through experience over time. When businesses treat people with the dignity they deserve, when they promote teamwork at the office, when they organize so that personal responsibility is optimized, and when they keep a firm eye toward the common good, then success follows. These principles are very pragmatic.

But hold on just a minute. Did I see a questioning look on your face? Ah, you've heard people talk about other Catholic social principles, such as the universal destination of goods and stewardship of the environment. Are you wondering why those principles aren't included in my list of four? Please rest assured that we are not ignoring them. Both ideas, as well as other principles often included in the comprehensive lists of Catholic Social Doctrine, are derivatives of one of the four core principles. In fact, both the universal destination of goods and environmental stewardship flow from the common-good principle.

Catholic Social Doctrine provides an updated, intellectually rigorous, and compelling system for ethical decision-making. It is based on natural law and virtue, but it takes those moral theories to new levels for moral guidance. In the remainder of this book, we will delve more deeply into this integrity-based approach and its guidance for business decision-making. But first, we need to spend a little more time on virtue, and that's the subject of the next chapter.

Questions for reflection

1. Think of an ethical decision that you participated in making. Which moral philosophy was used to make the decision—egoism, relativism, utilitarianism, virtue, or natural law? At the time of the decision, were you conscious of the different moral philosophies and which one you were employing?

2. Have you observed businesspeople who appear to follow an egoistic approach in their personal conduct? Have you observed businesses that appear to follow an egoistic approach? Did this result in problems?

3. If the goal of business is to provide products or services that make the world a better place in which to live, which moral philosophy provides the proper level of decision-making to make this happen?
4. Are you familiar with the body of writings known as Catholic Social Doctrine? Where did you learn about it? Does what you know about its principles—human dignity, solidarity, subsidiarity, and common good—make sense to you?

Chapter 4

Character Counts

*Excellence is an art won by training and habituation. We do
not act rightly because we have virtue or excellence, but we
rather have those because we have acted rightly. We are what
we repeatedly do. Excellence, then, is not an act but a habit.*

— Attributed to Aristotle

When the San Diego Padres drafted Matt LaChappa in 1993,
they had high hopes that the lanky left-handed player would
develop into a great pitcher. But in April 1996, while warming
up in the bullpen, LaChappa clutched his chest and collapsed
to the ground. He was having a heart attack. He survived
but suffered brain damage and has since been confined to a
wheelchair.

The Padres could have ended their contract with him, since
he was no longer able to fulfill his obligations on the mound.
Instead, they have continued to sign LaChappa to a minor-
league contract each year, for more than twenty years — thus
ensuring that he has income plus the health insurance he needs.
Fred Uhlman, vice president of the Padres offered this explana-
tion: "Professional sports are about wins and losses at the end
of the day, but for us it's more about people. This is just a story

about relationships, connections, and doing the right thing. Matt being a Padre for life is without a doubt the right thing."[55]

Integrity-based leadership requires that businesspeople have not only business skills but also outstanding moral character. Character refers to ongoing development in the virtues, both theological (faith, hope, and charitable love) and cardinal (prudence, justice, courage, and moderation). When confronted with ethical issues, those with well-developed character know which questions to ask and which considerations are most important in reaching a good decision.

In 2009, *Time* magazine proposed its list of the ten most corrupt CEOs (or "criminal executive officers").[56] The list was headed by Bernie Madoff, who ran a Ponzi-style investment operation that cheated clients out of $65 billion. Madoff admitted that he knew full well that what he was doing was unethical. He explained to the judge, "As I engaged in my fraud, I knew what I was doing was wrong, indeed criminal. When I began the Ponzi scheme, I believed I could end it shortly and I would be able to extricate myself and my clients from the scheme. However, this proved difficult, and as the years went by I realized that my arrest and [conviction] would eventually come."[57] Madoff knew that what he was doing was unethical. He knew that eventually he

---

[55] Kathy Schiffer, "San Diego Padre for Life: Team Continues Support for Disabled Former Pitcher," *National Catholic Register* Blog, April 2, 2017, http://www.ncregister.com/blog/kschiffer/san-diego-padre-for-life-team-continues-support-for-disabled-former-pitcher.

[56] "Top 10 Crooked CEOs," *Time*, http://content.time.com/time/specials/packages/article/0,28804,1903155_1903156_1903160,00.html.

[57] Brian Ross, *The Madoff Chronicles: Inside the Secret World of Bernie and Ruth* (New York: Hyperion, 2009), p. 208.

would get caught and pay the price for his crime, which turned out to be a 150-year prison term! Why didn't he step forward early on and admit his guilt?

Although we don't know for sure (and Bernie isn't talking), it appears that Madoff lacked the basic virtues of honesty and courage, and so was blocked from stepping forward to admit his lie. Sadly, he took the easier path and continued his deception until he was caught and his house of cards came crashing down around him.

Time's list of leading corrupt CEOs includes others who apparently knew right from wrong, including James McDermott of KBW, Sam Israel of the Bayou Group, and Bernie Ebbers of WorldCom. Like Madoff, they were weak in virtue and did not have the courage to admit their failings and make amends before their situations got out of hand.

As we look at the noteworthy ethical breaches that occur almost daily in business, we find that perpetrators of wrongdoing often know that what they are doing is wrong but lack the virtue to resist temptation. Accordingly, learning to become an integrity-infused leader is not solely about learning rules and standards. One must also become practiced in virtue. Many business schools err by ignoring character formation and its impact on ethics. Businesspeople must become familiar with the most important virtues and resolve to practice them.

What are virtues?

The *Catechism of the Catholic Church* defines virtues as "firm attitudes, stable dispositions, and habitual perfections of intellect and will that govern our actions, order our passions, and guide our conduct according to reason and faith" (no. 1804). There are theological virtues and human virtues. Theological virtues are the foundation of Christian moral activity and are infused by God into our souls at Baptism to make us capable of acting as His children and of meriting eternal life. There are three theological virtues: faith, hope, and charity.

- *Faith* is the theological virtue through which we believe in God and believe all that He has said and revealed to us, and that Holy Church proposes for our belief.

- *Hope* is the theological virtue by which we desire the kingdom of heaven and eternal life as our happiness, placing our trust in Christ's promises and relying not on our own strength, but on the help of the grace of the Holy Spirit.

- *Charity* is the theological virtue by which we love God above all things for His own sake, and our neighbor as ourselves. The practice of all the virtues is animated and inspired by charity, which binds everything together in perfect harmony. Charity upholds and purifies our human ability to love and raises it toward heavenly perfection.

The *Catechism* also provides very good information about human virtues, which are acquired by education, by deliberate acts, and by perseverance, ever renewed by divine grace. With God's help, they forge character and give facility in doing good things.

Four virtues—prudence, justice, courage, and moderation—play a pivotal role and accordingly are called *cardinal*; all the other virtues hinge on them.

- *Prudence* uses practical reason to discern our true good in every circumstance and to choose the right means of achieving it. Prudence is "right reason in action," writes St. Thomas Aquinas.

- *Justice* consists in the constant and firm will to give God and neighbor their due.
- *Courage* ensures firmness in difficulties and constancy in the pursuit of the good. The virtue of courage enables one to conquer fear, even fear of death, and to face trials and persecutions.
- *Moderation* (also called temperance) moderates the attraction of pleasures and provides balance in the use of created goods. It ensures the will's mastery over instincts and keeps desires within the limits of what is honorable.

Aristotle also described the cardinal virtues, or "hinge" virtues, as important aspects of personal character, necessary for virtuous relationships. The four cardinal virtues are important habitual ways for relating to various challenges in life: moderation helps us relate rightly to pleasure; courage to relate rightly to pain; justice to relate rightly to people; and prudence to relate rightly to truth.[58]

Why is virtue necessary for good business?

Earlier I mentioned that Pope Francis refers to business as a noble vocation. So, why does he say business is *noble*? Does he mean that businesspeople dress well and act like royalty? Well, not exactly. He is likely quoting St. Catherine of Siena, who said that it's not position, wealth, or appearance that makes a person noble; rather, it's virtue. A noble person is a virtuous person, one who is truthful, wise, just, and moderate. He or she is someone you can trust with all your heart!

---

[58] Chad Engelland, *The Way of Philosophy: An Introduction* (Eugene, OR: Cascade Books, 2016), p. 35.

Force for Good

When I was asked to serve as interim dean of the business school at the Catholic University of America, I thought it prudent to attend a seminar for new deans sponsored by the leading business school accreditation organization, the Association for the Advancement of Collegiate Schools of Business (AACSB). The seminar lasted two days and consisted of presentations by current and former educational leaders on what it takes to be successful as a business-school dean. One of the early presenters listed his top five keys to success, and the first key was "Never lie to your faculty." Later that day, another of the presenters stated, "My first recommendation to new deans is always be truthful to your faculty." The following day, a third dean repeated the same admonition about veracity and the probability that faculty will turn against you if you can't be trusted to tell the truth.

The fact that one dean made such a comment was curious. Shouldn't honesty go without saying? After all, it's one of the Ten Commandments. But the fact that three deans felt it was important enough to rank as their number-one recommendation is a sad indictment of today's society. Surprisingly, no one said anything about lying to administrators, staff, students, parents, donors, or alumni. Apparently, that's perceived to be okay, as long as you don't lie to faculty!

In order to be honest, one must be practiced in the cardinal virtues, which include prudence, justice, courage, and moderation. Prudence allows us to keep confidential information confidential; justice allows us to present information with sensitivity and respect for others affected; courage allows us to admit our failings and faults; and moderation allows us to rein in our excesses and provide balance in our discussions.

The army, the navy, the air force, and the marines conduct training camps with an eye toward character development so that recruits become schooled in the cardinal virtues. Recruits are put through physical and mental challenges in such a way that each learns prudence, justice, courage, and moderation while practicing teamwork and developing a high degree of trust in other team members. Individuals learn to do the right thing every time, even under stressful conditions. People of character make great business practitioners, and because veterans have undergone character training, they tend to be highly effective employees.

What happens when virtue is missing?

I remember my excitement a number of years back when I was invited to attend the quarterly marketing meeting for MCI/World-Com, which was then the largest telecommunications company in the world. The meetings were held in a large ballroom at a prominent Jackson, Mississippi, hotel not far from MCI/World-Com corporate headquarters in Clinton. One by one, marketing managers in charge of various divisions within the company were called to the front of the room. With elaborate PowerPoint presentations, they presented their divisions' quarterly performance as related to assigned goals.

When performance exceeded the goal, applause ensued. When performance was short of the goal, the room became tension-filled and very uncomfortable. Someone, usually the underperforming marketing manager's boss, would stand up and deliver a public tongue-lashing to the offending manager about the importance of achieving goals and reminding him or her that any further failures to achieve the assigned numbers would not be tolerated. There was no questioning whether conditions had changed or other factors had affected the outcome. It was all reduced to whether the numbers had been achieved or not. You were either a hero or a goat.

My host informed me that these public humiliations were an important means of promoting the virtue of goal orientation among managers. Anyone witnessing this spectacle would strongly desire to make sure that goals were achieved at all costs so that he or she would not be publicly embarrassed. I came away thinking that something was inherently wrong with this approach.

What was wrong? Certainly goal orientation is important for any manager to learn, and many regard it as a virtue, but if goal orientation is held as the highest of virtues—the one that trumps all other virtues—then the emphasis is potentially dangerous.

We know from the ancient Greeks, together with Christian tradition, that prudence, justice, courage, and moderation form the foundation of natural morality. These four must always be at the forefront in a manager's thinking, and all other virtues (except the theological virtues) should be secondary.

Fortunately, at least one manager didn't forget to apply the cardinal virtues in the MCI/WorldCom situation. Cynthia Cooper was employed in the audit department and demonstrated all four cardinal virtues when she stepped forward to blow the whistle on what turned out to be the most significant case of financial reporting fraud ever perpetrated. Prudence was needed to uncover the problem, justice to make sure that investors' rights were protected, moderation to keep her investigation hidden until it reached fruition, and courage to make the charges public in the face of company sanctions and personal threats.[59]

---

[59] Cynthia Cooper, *Extraordinary Circumstances: The Journey of a Corporate Whistleblower* (Hoboken, NJ: John Wiley and Sons, 2008).

As a result of Cynthia's adherence to the cardinal virtues, her testimony was able to stop an insider group directed by CEO Bernie Ebbers that had been doctoring the books so that it appeared that the company's financial goals were being met. Unfortunately, this group held goal orientation as their highest virtue. In 2005, Ebbers was convicted of fraud and sentenced to twenty-five years in prison. Cynthia Cooper wrote an outstanding book and today speaks to students and corporate groups about virtue.

The implications of Cynthia's story go further than revealing the company's fraud and ensuring that justice was achieved. Her story reveals to all of us that virtue is paramount to long-term success. As Aristotle once said, "Virtue makes us aim at the right mark, and practical wisdom makes us take the right means."[60] Had MCI/WorldCom aimed at the "right mark" of virtuous business rather than a win-at-any-cost mentality, perhaps they would not have found themselves in the situation that they did. If they had practiced the cardinal virtues, they might have achieved the long-run success that their CEO desired.

Which are the key virtues in business?

Social relationships can exist at three levels of goodness — pleasure, utility, and virtue.[61] In a pleasure relationship, each party seeks enjoyment from the other, and in a utility relationship, each expects something useful. Most business relationships are

---

[60] Aristotle, *Nicomachean Ethics in the Basic Works of Aristotle,* ed. Richard McKeon (New York: Random House, 1941), lines 935–1112.

[61] Engelland, *Way of Philosophy,* pp. 33–34.

modeled as one or the other. However, in a virtuous relationship, each individual not only receives some enjoyment and utility but also delights in the authentic character and basic goodness of the other.

Each individual comes to expect that the other will exercise virtue in all his or her dealings, and because each party sees the good in the other, each will correct the other if one ever makes a mistake. Virtues—and particularly the four cardinal virtues—allow the very best kind of relationships: the kind that are needed among coworkers to encourage beneficial change.

- *Moderation.* Businesspeople have a desire for pleasure —to win sales, gain promotions, dine at expensive restaurants, and be perceived to be among the elite at what they do. Moderation helps us avoid excess. Although pleasure has an allure, moderation takes control. Moderation allows us to enjoy pleasures without harm to ourselves, to our firms, or to others.

- *Courage.* Courage masters fear of pain. Businesspeople are sometimes reluctant to take a principled stand for fear of criticism from various stakeholders. But avoiding criticism or pain is not always the best course of action. We need a touch of bravery along with mental discipline to tough things out. Courage frees us and helps us overcome our aversion to pain by placing the potential pain in service of a genuine good.

- *Justice.* Justice (sometimes referred to as fairness) governs our right relationships with others. Often the difficulty in being just is controlling our tendencies to seek advantage at the expense of others. Justice jolts businesspeople out of their desires for advantage and invites them to see things from the perspective of others. This virtue shows us that our standards should be measured not by material success but by moral success.

• *Prudence* involves distinguishing ends from means, together with an ability to be attentive to the nature of things. Prudence gives businesspeople the grace to appreciate the true, the good, and the beautiful in their work. Without prudence they will lack insight and direction. Aristotle puts it this way: "Act in such a way that you treat humanity, whether in your own person or in the person of another, always at the same time as an end and never simply as a means." And further, "If he have not virtue, he is the most unholy and savage of animals, and the most full of lust and gluttony."[62]

One day I got a phone call from an executive search firm. The voice on the phone told me that the parent company of our leading competitor was impressed with what I had done and wanted to interview me for an executive vice president slot that was opening up in one of their noncompeting divisions. "Sure, I'd like to explore the opportunity," I said. The next week, I traveled to the competitor's location and met with the CEO of the parent company. I was prepared to talk about how my skills and experience could have an immediate impact in the new position. But the president's first question related to the marketing initiatives I was implementing in my current position, so I outlined them in very broad terms without revealing anything confidential. He then asked for specific details, and I explained that I was not willing to divulge such details to a competitor.

---

[62] Aristotle, *Politics*, in *The Basic Works of Aristotle*, ed. Richard McKeon (New York: Random House, 1941), lines 1127–1316.

He paused, leaned toward me, and said, "Your firm is out-maneuvering us in the marketplace, and it is imperative that I know how you are doing it."

Suddenly I realized that this interview was a charade. There was no opening for a vice president. He was asking me questions with the hope that I would reveal something confidential, something that his staff couldn't figure out.

"I wouldn't expect your executives to divulge trade secrets to a competitor, so I hope you don't expect me to do so either," I said as I walked out of his office.

I later found out that dangling job opportunities in front of managers at competing firms was a standard practice for this CEO. Apparently, there were many people who were duped into divulging information in the hopes of getting a better job. This is how he gained competitive intelligence that he couldn't get through legitimate means. But there is no virtue in this scheme. It is patently dishonest, unjust, and imprudent.

If we are to develop integrity-infused organizations, we need to work with colleagues who have high moral character, and that requires an understanding of both virtue and ethics. Business skill preparation needs to include some ethical literacy so that people will be wise to such subterfuge and dishonest CEOs will realize that they can't cheat this way. Unfortunately, however, many of our business schools are missing the mark by failing to provide ethical-literacy education.

What's wrong with ethics education today?

A false notion influences much of ethics education today — the notion that an individual's education about right and wrong is completed during childhood, and thus, his understanding of ethics is complete by the time he goes to college. Accordingly, colleges can't teach ethics—it is too late in the process—and the best we can hope for is to sensitize people to understand that there are many ideas about what is right and what is wrong.

This idea is false for two reasons. First, experience in working with college students has shown me that they are still developing morally and ethically and are actively testing their developing concepts of right and wrong. I've often seen that students will change their preconceptions after in-depth reading and in-class discussions. Second, since faculty have been successful in teaching a host of difficult and complex subjects to college students, there should be no reason why ethics can't also be taught.

Unfortunately, many college ethics classes have been structured with this false limitation in mind. Instead of teaching ethics, they teach students what various philosophers have recommended about ethical-decision rules, and they invite students to apply those decision rules to various structured ethical situations and cases. A diversity of viewpoints is encouraged so that students become adept at seeing situations from multiple perspectives. The result is that ethics becomes more of a conflict-resolution exercise than an integral decision-making process.

Andrew Abela has identified three weaknesses in ethics courses of this type: (1) they don't help students know *how* to be ethical; (2) they don't help students know *when* to be ethical; and (3) they don't help students know *why* to be ethical.[63] As a result, students end up categorizing ethics as an interesting side issue but not valid for helping guide business behavior.

---

[63] Andrew Abela, "What's Wrong with Business Ethics?" (presentation to the business faculty at the University of Malta, June 4, 2013).

Here's an example. Suppose your objective is to make the right decision—the correct *ethical* choice—about whether to capitalize or expense the cost of some new retail displays that are to be used for five years. Accounting standards require that revenues be matched with corresponding expenses in the same accounting period in which they occur, and sometimes retail displays are appropriately treated as capital equipment and amortized over their economic life.

Suppose you've just received an invoice for new retail displays that your company had agreed to amortize over five years. Suppose further that you've learned from a good customer that your leading competitor has a concept for new displays that will render yours quickly obsolete. It's too late to return these custom displays, and if they must be expensed this year, it will consume the entire expense budget for the year, leaving no room for other planned purchases. So, what is the ethical choice in this situation?

Should you tell your controller to expense this latest purchase because the displays are unlikely to be in use for the intended five years? Or should you wait until the competitor launches before you say something? Or transfer ownership of the displays to your subsidiary in Timbuktu? Or contact the competitor and make a deal with them so that they won't launch their new displays until the next fiscal year?

Unfortunately, the typical ethics course provides very little information that can help you through this ethical dilemma. The course might give you the definitions of different terms, instances of executives serving jail sentences for illegal activities, examples of how certain philosophers might look at ethical situations, and guidance about how people of different cultural backgrounds might have a different understanding regarding right and wrong.

But what you need is a listing of sound principles that help guide such decisions, together with a procedure for decision-making that ensures that all the important factors are considered. You need ethics coverage that is mainstreamed into all the core business courses, so that in accounting classes and marketing classes and finance classes, ethical considerations in those fields are covered in detail.

Naturally, your objective is to make the right decision every time decisions are made, and that means that ethical tests must be a regular part of the decision-making process. Stand-alone ethics courses often encourage students to believe that ethical considerations are a separate matter, not part of day-to-day business decisions. You need to be able to explain your decisions in such a way that the ethical rationale is clearly understood by all parties affected. This requires a reasoned and communicable analysis.

How can we fix ethics education?

A 2015 blog post entitled "I'm a Liberal Professor and My Liberal Students Terrify Me" created quite a bit of discussion on campuses across the nation. The author withheld his real name and academic affiliation, likely for fear of reprisals by the political left.

The basic thrust of the post was that many students have become so indoctrinated into today's secular culture that they are incapable of rational discussion or rational decision-making. Instead, their understanding about things that matter is based on personal feelings and emotion instead of on reasoned analysis. The author of the post lamented that when today's students are challenged to think, their first reaction is to run to the dean and complain that the professor doesn't respect them or the diversity that their perceptions and beliefs represent.

Why do I mention this blog post? A number of years ago, the business and economics faculty of CUA had the opportunity to lay the foundations for a new School of Business and Economics. The faculty were determined to create a different type of business school with business instruction that (1) was based on Catholic Social Doctrine, (2) had a vocational orientation (as in Pope Francis's remarks that "business is a noble vocation"), (3) incorporated a strong liberal-arts core, (4) integrated ethics across the curriculum, (5) championed character formation in virtue, and (6) met high standards for both practical and intellectual rigor. This was a bold initiative, quite different from what other business schools seemed to be doing.

The blog post reminded us that our university's original commitment to a liberal-arts orientation was based on a desire to help students learn to think clearly and express their ideas effectively so that they become model citizens in a vibrant world economy. But such an orientation must be balanced with a thorough education in the virtues, or we would all become terrified by the students we educate!

In the introduction to *The Book of Virtues*, William J. Bennett describes moral education as "the training of heart and mind toward the good"[64] and suggests that it involves explicit instruction, exhortation, training in good habits, and moral literacy. Moral literacy involves stories, poems, essays, and other writings that give individuals specific reference points about virtue. Stories speak to the inner part of an individual, to his or her moral sense. Consequently, storytelling is a very effective approach in

---

[64] William J. Bennett, *The Book of Virtues: A Treasury of Great Moral Stories* (New York: Simon and Schuster, 1993), p. 11.

conveying virtues to students, and stories need to be a part of a college curriculum that teaches virtue.

Virtue is an essential requirement for achieving happiness in this world, for developing beneficial human relationships, and for leading a productive organization.[65] Virtue informs ethical decision-making[66] and facilitates the development of good teamwork within an organization.[67] Virtue makes a person more effective in business.

Character formation through education in virtue was a major element of the university experience almost from the beginning. Over time, however, many universities broadened the goals of education toward students' cognitive success, while adding diversity, group equality, and multiculturalism components.[68] As additional nontraditional subjects became more prevalent in university education, something had to be eliminated to make room. That something was virtue. By the 1960s, our American higher-education system became severely compromised in its capacity to engage in virtuous character formation.[69]

---

[65] See Alexandre Havard, *Virtuous Leadership: An Agenda for Personal Excellence* (New York: Scepter Publishers, 2007).

[66] Mary Crossan, Daina Mazutis, and Gerard Seijts, "In Search of Virtue: The Role of Virtues, Values, and Character Strengths in Ethical Decision Making," *Journal of Business Ethics* 113, no. 4 (April 2013): 567–581.

[67] Brian Engelland, "Team-Building, Virtue, and Personal Flourishing in Organizations" (presented at Personal Flourishing in Organizations, Santa Croce University in Rome, February 24, 2014).

[68] See Carol Iannone, "What's Happened to Liberal Education?" *Academic Questions* (Winter 2003–2004): 54–66.

[69] See Allan Bloom, *The Closing of the American Mind* (New York: Simon and Schuster, 1987).

If universities don't act to fix ethics education soon, businesses will have to develop their own education programs for employees. ChildrenFirst, Inc. of Boston is an example of one firm doing just that (see "The Human Quality Initiative at ChildrenFirst, Inc.").

Another firm that places a high value on employee virtue is Koch Industries.[70] Koch has developed a hiring process designed to value virtue more than talent, and to identify and hire employees with outstanding moral character. CEO Charles Koch believes that such people will invariably become great employees and help the business prosper. A person with good character can usually develop the skills needed to succeed. Conversely, people with suspect character—even if they demonstrate good talent—can be corrosive to a company. Establishing a company culture that encourages strong character through virtue reinforcement is clearly a winning strategy.

Some universities are working to support this strategy. The Busch School of Business and Economics at the Catholic University of America saw this as an opportunity and began an initiative with four steps:

1. We identified eight core business courses and began to include virtue coverage into each one.
2. We increased the use of case analyses that transmit examples of virtue enacted by business role models.
3. We made efforts to increase the use of materials that showcase how integrity can be infused into organizations.

---

[70] See Charles G. Koch, *Good Profit: How Creating Value for Others Built One of the World's Most Successful Companies* (New York: Crown Publishing, 2015).

The Human Quality Initiative at ChildrenFirst, Inc.

"We have to do more than just professionally develop our employees," explained Rosemary Jordano, the founder and CEO of Boston-based ChildrenFirst, Inc., a provider of childcare services for Fortune 500 companies. "To be successful, we need to develop our employees so they have outstanding character."

Rosemary initiated a corporate-wide program seeking to educate employees in the human virtues most important to childcare success. The first task was to determine which human virtues to consider, so all two hundred employees were asked to identify three. Based on a tally of the results, the winners were patience, optimism, commitment, tolerance, and perseverance. It was easy to see that these virtues would be important in providing care to children, and they were accepted as those around which an educational program could be built. The program was called the "Human Qualities Initiative" (HQI) as the word "virtue" was criticized by some employees as being too religious.

Realizing that virtues must be practiced until they become habits, the initiative was scheduled to include both a "learn the quality" phase and a "practice the quality" phase. Consultants developed presentations on each of the five virtues, and once the education piece was finished, each department determined how that quality might best be practiced in its area.

At the end of the first year, the entire company met to review progress toward including the virtues in all aspects of their work. The next two years were spent making the HQI part and parcel of everything the company did, from serving children in its centers, to greeting visitors and callers, to meeting with sales prospects. Programs were introduced to welcome new employees to the company, and to bring them up to speed.

Positive results were noted in three areas: recruiting, turnover, and client satisfaction. The company realized that having a culture in which employees were explicitly committed to personal improvement was a significant attraction. It began to promote the HQI in its advertising and trained its recruiting staff to discuss the program in interviews.

Childcare is a high-turnover industry, and any reduction in the turnover rate can yield substantial savings. At CFI, the teacher turnover rate was approximately 60 percent before the program began. At the end of three years, that rate had declined to 40 percent, due in part to the HQI. Since fewer new employees had to be recruited to replace departing ones, the savings in recruiting and training costs amounted to approximately $200,000 each year.

Today, the HQI has become engrained in the company's culture. It is described in company brochures, is included in job interviews, is part of every training session, and is enshrined in the play activities of children in the centers. Even their parents have noticed the impact and have asked if they, too, can participate in the HQI ("I could use a little more patience").*

*Information about this company was provided by William Bowman, former president of CFI.

4. We sought to increase the number of internship opportunities available to our students in integrity-infused organizations.

In the following paragraphs, I'd like to relate some of the specific actions we undertook to integrate virtue education into our program.

Virtue Coverage in the Core Business Courses
The faculty were determined that virtue education not be limited to one course, but be incorporated into a significant number of courses spread over all four years of the student's BSBA degree program. Accordingly, faculty identified seven courses, including the first business course students take as freshmen (the Vocation of Business), the last course students take as seniors (Business Strategy) and five other business courses that are required in the business core and normally taken by sophomores and juniors (Introduction to Accounting, Management Theory, Business Law, Business Ethics, and Marketing Management). These seven courses represent 38 percent of all the courses in the business core and enable the coverage of virtue to pass the tipping point.

Force for Good

Initially, the dean asked each of the twelve faculty members involved in teaching these courses to explore how they might cover virtue more effectively in their course, and these faculty responded in a variety of ways. Six added virtue education as a learning objective and incorporated the topic multiple times throughout the semester as a significant part of the course. Four more members included the virtue topic in two or more classes, and two others added at least one lecture. Most faculty added supplementary readings—either books or selected chapters—and a listing prepared in 2016 included fifteen titles. Faculty also found various other materials to convey the topic, adding book chapters, articles, video clips, and cases to enhance classroom discussion and student learning.

• *Examples of virtue enacted by business leaders.* Name just about any field of study—philosophy, physics, literature—and most of the students majoring in it will be able to identify several great contributors to that field. But in the field of business, it is different. Business faculty often talk about successful companies while integrating case studies into their classes, but they don't spend much time discussing individuals. Although business has its share of outstanding leaders who have transformed ideas into great works, a review of popular business texts suggests that little attention is paid to individuals who can serve as role models for the virtues and personal characteristics they employed in their working life. To fill this void, business faculty have begun collecting stories about the struggles and accomplishments of some of these great business leaders, and using them to illustrate the qualities needed for real-world business success. Students really appreciate gaining the perspective that these stories provide, and they learn about virtue in the process.

• *Use of materials that showcase virtuous management.* Cases, class exercises, projects, and videos may all be used to convey virtues in business.[71] At CUA's Busch School of Business and Economics, the first course that business majors take, called the Vocation of Business, requires students to form a simple Internet-based business in which they provide Web content, attract visitors to their website, and earn click-through fees from firms such as Amazon.com when visitors move from the student website to a commercial site. In setting up this micro business, students go through all the steps usually required to begin a business, including making decisions about mission and objectives. The course instructor requires all students to assess how the cardinal virtues play a role in these decisions.

Thus, freshmen get an early introduction to virtue in an applied way. Other cases and exercises are incorporated throughout the core curriculum as students move through the program. Even business cases not specifically designed with a virtue component can be modified by adding discussion questions that apply to virtue. For instance, when discussing a case about a marketing problem, the instructor can ask questions such as, "If the decision-maker was motivated by fairness, which alternative would she select?" or "Does the behavior of the principal reflect the virtue of moderation? Why or why not?"

Faculty completed a survey to assess which virtues they were covering in their core business classes, and a compilation of these results indicates that the virtues discussed most frequently included persistence, perseverance, courage, truthfulness, curiosity,

---

[71] Stephen M. Mintz (1996), "Aristotelian Virtue and Business Ethics Education," *Journal of Business Ethics* 15, no. 8 (1996): 827–838.

honesty, industry, and self-reliance. Students are all required to take and pass comprehensive exams at the end of their degree program, and in the future, those exams will include a virtue component.

Internships in Virtuous Organizations
Good internship experiences are helpful in giving students real-world business experiences that help them understand business processes more completely. When the internship is with a virtuous firm, the experience is even more valuable. The Busch School has a full-time internship coordinator who seeks out and identifies good businesses as opportunities for internships. Students are normally required to write a paper on their internship experience, including an assessment of the firm's ethical character. Based on these student assessments over time, the faculty expect to learn which internship businesses offer the most virtuous experiences so that they can advise students appropriately.

Virtue is an old idea that is making a strong comeback, and it's about time! Team members who work on developing virtue each day become more adept at treating others with respect and justice. This translates into the development of fruitful relationships with employees, customers, and society at large. In the next three chapters, we'll look integrity in each of these relationships.

Questions for reflection

1. Think about your character. What influences and people have shaped it? Do you continue to work on developing your character? How do you do so?

2. It has been said that a person's character is best re-vealed when no one is looking. Do you possess two characters — one for public consumption and another hidden from others? Does the public character change depending on who is watching? Do you know persons who act as if they possess multiple characters?

3. If your colleagues were asked to name your virtues, which ones would they name? Which vices might they name?

4. Suppose you wanted to improve your performance on one virtue. Which would you select, and what steps would you take to improve?

5. Think of a business with which you are familiar. Which virtues should the business possess to be suc-cessful? How can this business "move the needle" so that more employees demonstrate the virtues needed for success?

Chapter 5

Integrity-Infused Employee Relationships

*Business as vocation helps us understand that the gifts that God
has given—and we all have different gifts—are to be used for the
benefit of others. In doing so, we co-create with God in providing
goodness for our families, our customers, and our communities.*

—Tim Busch, founder and CEO of the Pacific Hospitality Group, "Better Business Education"

In chapter 3 we discussed the four key principles that provide
for integrity: human dignity, solidarity, subsidiarity, and the
common good. The application of these principles in business
provides some interesting and sometimes surprising conclusions
about how we should operate. In this chapter, we look at how
these principles apply to the workplace, and in the next two,
we'll extend them to customer relationships and the competitive environment.

What is the distinctive character of work?

In the 1963 movie *McLintock!*, John Wayne plays a wealthy
rancher named G. W. McLintock, and Wayne's son Patrick plays
a young cowhand down on his luck and seeking a job. McLintock

hires the cowhand, and the young man expresses appreciation for being given the job. But McClintock replies in bombastic Wayne fashion, "Why, I'm not givin' you nuttin'! This is an even trade. You're turnin' in a hard day's work, and I'm payin' a fair day's wage. No more and no less!"

This scene is helpful in demonstrating the difference between the objective and subjective natures of work. John Wayne's character is viewing work based on its objective nature, in which the worker does something of value—such as feeding horses, mending a fence, or branding cattle. But there's a more important aspect to work. That's the aspect that Patrick Wayne's character discerns.

This more important aspect of work is its subjective nature. Our work is an essential expression of our human nature as created in the image and likeness of God. St. John Paul II explained it in this way: "Work is good for man ... because through work, man not only transforms nature but he also achieves fulfillment as a human being."[72]

God is the great Creator—He created the heavens and the earth and all who dwell in it—and we humans like to imitate God by creating things with the talents and capabilities we've been given. We work with our minds to figure things out, and work with our hands to create things of beauty or add our own touch to the things that God has given to us. The subjective nature of work allows us to exercise our God-given creativity by learning new skills, gaining insights, making friends, enhancing self-esteem, and becoming more than we were before the work began. Consequently, our work forges beneficial changes in us and makes us better off than we were before the work began.

---

[72] John Paul II, *Laborem Exercens*, no. 9.

St. John Paul II explains further: "Man, created in the image of God, shares by his work in the activity of the Creator. Within the limits of his own human capabilities, man continues to develop that activity and perfects it as he advances further and further in the discovery of the whole of creation."[73]

Our work not only assists our personal growth but also allows us to influence the attitudes of the people around us and to shape our world. Accordingly, the subjective dimension is more important than the objective dimension; the worker is more important than the work.

The principle of human dignity requires a different perspective than is required by classical economics. What we call capital, which is wealth in the form of money or other assets, represents the accumulation of the results of work. We work, we earn, we save, and hopefully we accumulate capital. Now, here's the point: the principle of human dignity requires that the worker is significantly more important than capital, and therefore human labor cannot be considered as merely another factor in production.

Workers are entitled to certain innate rights that capital is not accorded. These include the right to just compensation, the right to work, the right to rest, the right to safe working conditions, and the right to associate with other workers for collective-bargaining purposes. These rights are necessary to enable the integral development of the whole human person — in other words, development of mind, body, and spirit. Firms that work to provide these rights have the opportunity to develop a high-quality workforce, one that achieves outstanding productivity and efficiency.

[73] Ibid.

Force for Good

I asked a restaurant owner why his business wasn't open on Sundays. He explained that his restaurant concept required a high degree of personal service, and that, to achieve and maintain that high degree, he needed to hire and retain good employees. But none of his good employees wanted to work on Sundays—they wanted to spend time at home with their families. By implementing his "closed on Sunday" policy, he believes his service quality is higher and his training and retention costs are lower than those of his competitors who are open every day. Consequently, he believes his profitability is higher even though he operates only six days per week.

Because we humans are called to work, human dignity requires that anyone capable of working should not be denied the opportunity for gainful employment. This means that businesses should appropriately be encouraged to grow so as to create more opportunities for good employment, and to provide effective development of employees so that they may increase their potential and assist in the firm's growth.

But firms don't act alone. Human dignity requires that governmental entities have a responsibility in this regard. State authority is required to structure a sound economic system that encourages employment and economic growth. And one other thing that all aspects of society, including the workplace, need is the feminine genius. The presence of women in the workplace helps support the common good.[74]

Another vital worker right is the right to adequate physical rest and rejuvenation. Workers should be granted sufficient rest and free time so that they may tend to their family, cultural, social, and religious life. As Pope Leo XIII famously stated:

[74] Pontifical Council for Justice and Peace, *Compendium*, no. 295.

It is neither just nor human so to grind men down with excessive labor so as to stupefy their minds and wear out their bodies.... Strength is developed and increased by use and exercise, but only on condition of due intermission and proper rest.[75]

Finally, the job environment and all manufacturing processes should not be harmful to the worker's physical health or moral integrity. This is a matter of human dignity.

Mark Weber is the former president of the public sector at NetApp, considered one of the best firms to work for in America. Mark told me that NetApp showed respect for people not only in hiring actions but also in terminations. Getting a pink slip is a dehumanizing process in some companies. The discharged employee is immediately required to turn in his ID card, his office keys, and his parking pass and told he must clear out his personal items and leave within thirty minutes. An armed security guard then stands over the discharged employee as he grabs his belongings and leaves the building. Human resource directors tell me that this is done to prevent the employee from damaging or stealing something in revenge for the termination.

But NetApp follows a different approach. "We hire, train, coach, evaluate, and then coach again," Mark explained. "If it ever reaches the point when someone must be terminated, the employee has known about their inadequate performance for a significant period of time. We treat the departing meeting as an opportunity to allow those people to exit with grace. We help them find other jobs so that they can continue to hold our company in high regard as enthusiastic supporters of what we do."

---

[75] Leo XIII, Encyclical *Rerum Novarum*, May 15, 1891, no. 42.

Force for Good

Good coaching requires frequent feedback so that employees always know how their performance is viewed. If someone comes to work wearing yoga pants, the supervisor needs to inform that employee privately why such attire is inappropriate for the office. Human dignity requires that such conversations are kept private and confidential.

I recall one employee who came to me frequently to criticize another employee's productivity and work ethic. I thanked that employee for her concern and information, but I cautioned her that respect for human dignity required that I not divulge anything about my conversations and coaching of the employee she was complaining about. I then turned it into a coaching session and showed her what she could do to help the other team member improve her performance. Initially, she balked because she was more interested in discussing other people's performance than her own. But eventually she came around and helped raise the performance of her coworkers.

When employers are not forthcoming in recognizing human dignity, integrity requires that workers be allowed to form unions, or associations that defend their vital work-related interests. Relationships between unions and companies should be cooperative, not adversarial. Unions have a further responsibility to help educate workers about their role in and impact on the economy. When union demands put companies in uncompetitive economic positions, everyone loses.

Should employers still shirk their responsibilities, then it is appropriate for the state to step in and pass protective legislation. In the United States, numerous laws have been enacted to protect employees, including laws that promote affirmative action, civil rights, immigration, collective bargaining, equal pay, social security, and safety and health; and additional laws that reduce age discrimination, child labor, and sex discrimination and attempt to promote appropriate compensation.

What is just compensation?

To understand compensation, let's to turn to Pope Leo XIII's 1891 encyclical *Rerum Novarum*. In it, Pope Leo upheld private property as a sacred right, condemned socialism, condemned revolution and violent action, and provided an indirect endorsement of capitalism. All this was pretty radical for that time! But the encyclical did something else that began a controversy that continues to this day. It established the concept of a just wage.

Leo defined a just wage as the amount needed to provide current support and long-term savings for a thrifty worker and his family without having to put either spouse or children to work at paid labor. Savings was necessary, Leo reasoned, so that the family breadwinner could eventually accumulate property that could be used to cover the expenses of life should illness or injury prevent him or her from continuing to work. Leo considered this to be a moral argument and left it to the economists to work out the details. Economists have been arguing ever since.

You see, classic economics reduces all economic questions to a science of free exchanges, a science that eliminates all questions of distributive justice. The cost of labor is based upon the equilibrium between supply and demand. If the pay isn't high enough, the worker withholds his work until the pay is raised enough to make it worth his while. If the individual worker demands too much pay, the company finds another who is willing to work at the offered pay rate.

But along came this encyclical, saying that that approach is not moral or just. Why not? Leo understood an important aspect of human nature. Men and women like to imitate the Creator by using their talents and skills to create things, albeit on a much smaller scale. We don't like to sit around and do nothing. Rather, we like to get up and accomplish something with our time and skills. People have a strong propensity to work, and we seek to work even if no one will pay us for it.

Now, don't misunderstand. Sure, you know someone who won't get out of bed until noon and never does a lick of work! But that person is an outlier. Most people are not averse to work itself but are averse to work performed under degrading or oppressive conditions. When work is boring or repetitive, or requires no exercise of the mind, or doesn't receive recognition for the contribution it makes, we likely will try to avoid it. We don't want to be treated like a robot.

Leo recognized that men and women will readily agree to work for low wages or even no wages, just so they can exercise their God-given creative talents. Leo also knew that a labor rate negotiation, like all negotiations, all too often becomes a power struggle rather than a fair negotiation. The stronger party gets the better deal. Since a large employer tends to have the power, "free bargaining" is not really so free and rarely results in a fair exchange. Capital tends to be overcompensated. So, if "free exchange" doesn't work when determining a just wage, what can work?

How do we determine a "just wage?"

The four principles of integrity can be applied to provide guidelines for just-wage determination.

First, the principle of human dignity (people first) requires that wages should be sufficient to cover the typical obligations of the wage earner's life, with enough left to save for a rainy day.[76] Second, the principle of solidarity (teamwork) requires that wages should be sustainable and within the normal economic capabilities of the firm.[77] Third, the principle of subsidiarity (personal responsibility) requires that wages should take into consideration the differences in preparation and skills necessary for different positions, together with individual worker contributions to the enterprise, so that the more difficult positions merit higher pay.[78] Finally, the common good (human flourishing) requires that wages are set at levels that can support a robust economy that produces employment opportunities for everyone who desires work.[79]

Implementation of these guidelines is clearly the responsibility of the employer, and firms have the moral obligation to gather sufficient data so that their wage levels can be set appropriately. This might require periodic studies to determine whether (1) employees are able to accumulate savings at the current wage rate, (2) wage levels are competitive with other employment opportunities in the area, and (3) prevailing wages are sufficient to support the general economic activity in the communities where employment occurs. This level of analysis requires thoughtful introspection and attention to detail.

Some employers don't agree with this level of moral responsibility. They argue that once an employee signs an employment contract to do certain work for a certain pay level, the fairness of the wage rate has already been established. There is no need for

---

[76] John Paul II, *Laborem Exercens*, no. 19.

[77] John XXIII, *Mater et Magistra*, no. 71.

[78] Vatican Council II, Pastoral Constitution on the Church in the Modern World *Gaudium et Spes*, December 7, 1965, no. 67.

[79] John XXIII, *Mater et Magistra*, no. 71.

subsequent periodic analysis. But this argument fails to consider human nature and our innate desire to work, a motivation that overwhelms our interest in negotiating a good deal and biases our individual judgment.

If we were negotiating the sale of a car or house and didn't like the first price offered, we could hold off selling and wait until a higher bid comes forth. But when there are mouths to feed and bills to pay, we can't logically withhold our labor while waiting for a better offer. Our negotiating position is very weak. Agreement between the two parties is not sufficient to provide moral justification for the wage amount.[80] The employer must structure pay levels so that workers are not penalized for this negotiating weakness. Pope Leo put it this way: "If through necessity or fear of a worse evil the workman accepts harder conditions because an employer or contractor will afford him no better, he is made the victim of force and injustice."[81]

Remember, the moral obligation is to pay a just wage, not the going rate that may be indicated by market forces. It is mistaken to avoid paying a just wage when it is higher than the going rate by arguing that this reduces profits and takes from the shareholders what is rightfully theirs. Paying a just wage is a moral obligation, and therefore it belongs to the employee even before it is granted to him or her in a paycheck. Shareholders do not have a right to benefit from paying less than just wages to employees.

The responsibility for ensuring just wages is shared by the state.[82] The principle of subsidiarity requires that laws and regulations should provide a facilitating environment for business

---

[80] *Catechism of the Catholic Church* (CCC), no. 2434.
[81] Leo XIII, *Rerum Novarum*, no. 45.
[82] John Paul II, *Laborem Exercens*, no. 15.

operation so that businesses thrive, employ workers, pay just wages, and create products and services that make the world a better place. The principle of solidarity requires that the state should ensure that safety nets are made available to workers who become injured or otherwise find themselves between jobs.

However, neither of the principles indicates which entity should operate these programs, and both private and public solutions have been employed over the years. In the United States, we've opted for a combination of industry associations, state agencies, and state-run unemployment compensation payments to address these needs.

Are differences in pay ethical?

When I last checked, LeBron James was paid $77 million per year as a basketball player for the Cleveland Cavaliers; Ralph Lauren was paid $67 million as the CEO of the company that bears his name; Ann Snyder was paid $47,500 as a market researcher for a restaurant supply house; and Jason Alexander was paid $13,220 as a cashier at McDonald's restaurant. Can we say that any of these wages are just?

LeBron James's salary is one of the highest for athletes, and Ralph Lauren's salary ranks as one of the highest salaries for a CEO, but we should not begrudge them for their good fortune. Although neither wage is justifiable based on need, and it's a stretch to say that either is based on equity, since most CEOs and baseball stars are paid far less, a case can be made that these extreme wages are justifiable based on economic order. After all, Ralph Lauren has provided effective leadership to establish a very successful brand, and the Cleveland Cavaliers are one of the winningest basketball teams with LeBron in the lineup. These extreme pay levels, however, would be a violation of economic order should they cause the organization to struggle financially; and it certainly would be morally wrong if the high pay level of one employee required cutting back another employee's pay so that it became less than just pay.

The market researcher's wages look pretty good in comparison, until you realize that they are $20,000 less than what a competitor pays its employees for the same work. Still, the first firm is justified in paying less than the competitor if the company can demonstrate that paying a just wage is unsustainable due to the firm's precarious financial health. If this pay inequity continues after the firm has attained good financial health, however, it would strain credibility to say that financial difficulties are the primary reason for the pay inequity.

Regarding the cashier, if this young man lives in a city with a high cost of living, such as New York, his wages are likely insufficient to pass the needs test and are unjust. Businesses have a responsibility to estimate how much employees need in order to handle their responsibilities in the geographic area where the business operates, and to pay wages accordingly.

Most of the time, the just-pay problem occurs at the lower end of the pay scale. Reell Manufacturing Company, a Silicon Valley manufacturer of injection-molded computer parts, wanted to make sure that the pay scales they were using to hire employees did in fact meet the standards of need, equity, and economic order so that their wages could be considered just.[83]

---

[83] Michael Naughton and David Specht, *Leading Wisely in Difficult Times: Three Cases of Faith and Business* (Mahwah, NJ: Paulist Press, 2011).

After evaluating the cost of living in the area, typical employee family sizes, and other economic factors, the management team was disappointed to find out that the pay rate for one class of workers was less than just pay required. Further, if the company did pay a just wage, it would add costs that would place the company in a noncompetitive position.

Often, a solution can be found by redesigning the job, and that's what Reell decided to do. By delegating more authority to the individual worker, less supervision and fewer support functions were needed. This upgrade reduced overhead costs and made it economically possible to pay a just wage for this class of workers.

How does an employer develop an employee's full potential?

So far, we've discussed what a company should do for employees, but integrity requires reciprocity in the employer-employee relationship. Employees have a responsibility to serve as effective partners in achieving the goals of the business, taking advantage of opportunities to develop their skills and to become increasingly more effective in the work necessary for success. The great untapped source of economic growth is not physical capital, but human capital leveraged by the creativity and dedication that workers bring to work each day.

But modern firms often have difficulty taking full advantage of this source of growth, for three reasons: (1) ineffective leadership, (2) stifling job design, and (3) poorly designed incentives. Leadership involves achieving personal and organizational greatness by bringing out the greatness in others.[84] The secret

---

[84] Havard, *Virtuous Leadership*.

Applying Subsidiarity at Nucor Corporation

Subsidiarity involves hiring the right people, getting them the tools they need to do the job, incentivizing them appropriately, and then getting out of their way. It is a simple idea that the steel-making company Nucor seems to have implemented to perfection.

Nucor's organization structure is lean and decentralized, with only four management layers. "We have a very flat organization structure," said a former president. "The standard joke in the company is that if you are a janitor and you get five promotions, you'll have the president's job."*

Each of the firm's twenty-five plants operates as if it were an independent business. "We are honest-to-God autonomous," said the general manager of one plant. "That means that we often inadvertently duplicate efforts made in other parts of Nucor. The company might develop solutions to the same problem six times. But the innovation advantages of local autonomy are so great, we think it is worth it."**

Employee relations at Nucor are based on four principles: (1) wages based on productivity, (2) no layoffs, (3) fair treatment, and (4) easy appeals.

---

*Richard Franklin, "An Interview with John D. Correnti, President and CEO of Nucor Corporation," *Wall Street Journal Corporate Reporter*, September 9–15, 1996, p. 20.
**Ken Iverson, *Plain Talk: Lessons from a Business Maverick* (Hoboken, NJ: John Wiley and Sons, 1998), p. 27.

Employees appreciate the firm's commitment not to lay off employees in periods when business is down. Instead of the usual industry practice of reducing the work force, Nucor reduces the work week for all.

The company's labor force was not unionized. An employee at Nucor in Hickman, Arkansas, presented the majority view: "Why is Nucor nonunion? I see two main reasons. First, it's just not needed. Nucor takes very good care of its employees. Its pay and benefits package is top-notch. No one has been capriciously fired. There are no layoffs. Nucor listens to its employees through monthly crew meetings, annual dinners, and employee surveys. We just don't need union mediators.... The second reason is that we all work together. We don't need divisiveness. We don't need adversaries. We can talk among ourselves and work out our own problems."*

*Claude Riggin, "Freedom and a Hell of a Lot More at Nucor," *New Steel* (July 1996).

to obtaining the faithful collaboration of employees is for the boss to exemplify the two most important leadership virtues: magnanimity and humility. Magnanimity can be defined as the realization that your talents are a gift from God and are valuable only when they are used to help others become better at what they do. Humility is the conviction that everyone is a gift from God and Christ is present in the least of them. Magnanimity and humility are virtues specific to leaders.

Force for Good

One day I got a call from the legal counsel of the firm where I worked to inform me that one of my direct reports had been accused of sexual harassment by another employee. The counsel told me that I must take steps to prevent the two employees from having contact with each other until an investigation could be conducted. Further, I was told that I could not say anything about the matter to either employee. I asked what the accused had done, and he told me that it was confidential. I asked whether the accused employee would be informed of the charges, and the counsel said, "Absolutely not! If he knows about the investigation, he can threaten the witnesses and we won't be able to get the testimony we need."

"I thought that people were innocent until proven guilty," I explained. "Doesn't he get to defend himself?"

"Not when the charge is sexual harassment," was his reply. "The first priority is to protect the accuser, and the second priority is to protect our company. The accused comes in as a distant third." Obviously, the legal counsel was concerned about keeping our company from being named in a lawsuit. That was his job.

But this troubled me greatly. Leadership is supposed to practice virtue first, not damage control. Magnanimity suggested that we needed to treat those two employees with care and tenderness so that their dignity would be respected and they would become better employees. Humility suggested that there may have been something else going on that we didn't yet understand.

I called the human resource professional who was charged with conducting the investigation and encouraged her to conduct her review promptly and with compassion. I also gave her the names of other people who might be able to shed light on the incident.

When all the testimony had been gathered, I was pleased to learn that the incident was more of a misunderstanding than a case of real harassment. The accuser was new to the department. The accused had told a joke in mixed company, and the accuser took it the wrong way and was offended. But she did not tell the accused, or anyone else, that she didn't want to hear such jokes again; she simply filed the harassment complaint with our counsel. When the accused was informed that such jokes were not appreciated, he promised not to do such a thing again, and when the accuser was informed that it would be a good idea to communicate disapproval when something happens that is offensive, she agreed to do so. As a result of this incident, both became better employees.

When employees perceive that the leader of their workplace is offering the opportunity to help them perfect their individual capacities, to engage in work that is useful and profitable, and to contribute according to their abilities to the service of the community, they respond in kind. Employees can feel compelled to adopt some of the boss's energizing spirit.[85] And this spirit will continue as long as the job they are asked to perform is structured so that it remains invigorating.

The usual approach to job design is based on scientific-management concepts pioneered by Frederick Taylor.[86] The idea behind scientific management is that there is a one "best way" to perform any job. By researching the best way, training employees in the best way, and then insisting that the best way be performed

---

[85] Pope Paul VI (1956), Address of Pope Paul VI to the First National Congress of Small Industry (January 20, 1956).

[86] Claude S. George, Jr. (1968), *The History of Management Thought*, Englewood Cliffs, NJ: Prentice-Hall, Inc., pp. 138–141.

each and every cycle, a business can optimize the effectiveness of the labor performed. Unfortunately, implementation can result in routinized jobs that becomes mindless and boring and non-thinking employees with diminished capacity for creativity and innovation. This is not a good result.

In the last twenty years, a different approach to job design began emerging that takes advantage of the principle of subsidiarity. It is called the human-centered approach, and it takes both technology and human needs into consideration in the job-design process.

The human-centered approach enables individual workers to participate so that the worker has an influence on the use of technology, not the other way around. Rather than insisting that the employee follow a job-design expert's tightly scripted set of motions for completing a task, managers might offer the employee a chance to experiment in developing his or her own alternative procedures to get the job done. This allows the employee to change the way the job gets done and to reduce the mind-numbing boredom induced by repetitive operations.

When employees have a strong voice in developing a job, they incorporate variety so that the job maintains their interest and attention. As a result, employees are more engaged in getting the work accomplished, and the employer is rewarded with a more collaborative and creative workforce.

Creating the proper incentives is the third area where firms struggle. For some jobs, it is easy and straightforward to develop appropriate incentives. A bricklayer should lay a certain number of bricks per day, and when that number is surpassed, the employee deserves additional pay. But for managers, the job becomes much more complex. The incentive needs to consider all the important aspects of the job, including productivity, safety, and employee relations.

General Motors: Learning from Employees

"It's totally unfair!" exclaimed Darlene. "The conveyor moves faster past my station than it does past all the others."

Darlene was an assembly operator assigned to station 3 on the Cadillac wiring-harness assembly line at the General Motors assembly plant in Warren, Ohio. I was the line-start follow-up specialist charged with helping to train operators and getting the line up to production speed, and I had just asked Darlene why she was having difficulty.

"Darlene, the conveyor is connected all the way around, so it has to run at the same speed past all the stations," I explained. "Here, I'll show you."

I pulled out my stopwatch and timed the conveyor past the second station, past the fourth station, and then past her station. I showed her the readings each time, and the times were all identical.

"Your stopwatch is wrong!" she cried.

We were getting nowhere. "Look, Darlene, how can we make your station work?" I asked. "We need to get this line up to design speed," I continued.

Darlene then requested that one of the supply fixtures be moved to a position about three inches lower and to the right. This didn't make any sense to me. The engineers had designed the station so as to minimize the amount of motion required by the operator to grab the lead, plug it into a connector, and then string it across the fixture. Any changes in the supply-fixture position would increase the time required to perform the necessary operations at the station. But I was ready to try anything. I asked the mechanic to reposition the fixture to where Darlene wanted it.

When I returned, I was amazed at what I saw. With the repositioned fixture in place, Darlene was now doing two of the required operations at the same time in synchronized precision. This wasn't the way the station had been designed, but Darlene was now performing all the required grabs, pulls, and plugs and getting it all done with plenty of time to spare. The line was now running at full design speed.

I learned something. People, even the difficult ones, have good ideas about what needs to be done in their workspace, and when they are given the opportunity to control that space, they know how to organize it for effective performance.

With new respect, I said, "Well done, Darlene! Is there anything else you need to make this line run right?" And she told me several other improvements she wanted made.

I know of a company whose plant manager was paid a salary plus an incentive bonus based on on-time shipment of customer orders. The company had just completed the development of a new proprietary product for a Canadian customer that would represent a major business opportunity. Prototypes of the product had been approved by the customer and the Canadian standards authority, and the customer had placed a huge order.

To meet the shipping promise date, the plant was scheduled for overtime. Unfortunately, scale-up didn't go smoothly, and the product coming off the line was slightly out of spec in one area. The plant manager had to decide whether to shut everything down and wait for the engineers to solve the problem, or finish producing the product, even though it was slightly out of spec. This manager wanted the bonus, and the out-of-spec condition seemed to be minor, so he completed the order and shipped it ... with disastrous consequences. The "minor" out-of-spec condition meant that none of the product met Canadian government standards, and all of it was rejected. The customer was not very happy and switched to a competitor. Had the plant manager's compensation been based on on-time shipping of in-spec product, this problem may have been avoided.

Why does integrity require information sharing among employees?

Mark Twain said, "Figures never lie, but liars figure," and this is a somber warning to those with jobs as financial analysts, engineers, and statisticians. It is very easy to slip into the mind-set that your job is not to seek the truth, but to present information to support the boss's presupposed conclusion.

Political polling during the 2016 presidential election is a good example of this mind-set. Many national polltakers adjusted what they reported so as to support the preconceived notion that the Democratic candidate had a better organization than the Republican candidate and would turn out a greater percentage of the electorate in battleground states. This turned out to be an erroneous preconception.

If employees are expected to exercise personal responsibility, then truth does have value and companies need to open the flow of information so that employees and managers at all levels have the facts they need to carry out their responsibilities. One of my students worked an internship at a financial-services company and came to me in an agitated state of mind. "Now I understand what you meant by the free flow of information within an organization!" he lamented. "My boss won't let me share with other managers the customer purchase information I've just collected," he continued. "He wants to wait until the quarterly director's meeting to reveal it so he can look good in front of the directors."

A friend gave me an example of what can happen when information is withheld. Apparently, his company's corporate headquarters had decided to combine a low-performing division with a high-performing one, figuring that the management team in the high-performing division could run both operations and turn around the failing one in the bargain. My friend was the analysist charged with helping to determine whether the new divisional headquarters would remain in its current location or move to the location of the failing division.

My friend analyzed the short-term and long-term cost impacts of each location and then recommended that the headquarters stay put so as to avoid significant relocation, hiring, and training costs, if existing managers were not willing to move. The new division president, however, had my friend remove much of these cost impacts, based on the supposition that key employees would all be delighted to assume their expanded responsibilities in a different city. That changed the analysis, which now clearly favored the move, and that was the analysis that was submitted to corporate for their approval.

When the consolidation began, only three of twelve members of the management team were willing to move their families to another city. The others immediately took jobs with other companies. The firm was forced to fill the positions with managers from the failing division, and the performance of the combined division immediately suffered. Within twelve months, the division president took a job in another industry, and after three more years of mediocre performance, the combined division was sold to the leading competitor.

What happened? My friend found out later that the president's wife grew up in the city where the failing division was located. She wanted to move back there, and her husband structured the analysis to convince headquarters that moving there was a good idea. Headquarters had been given meaningless data, and it ended up hurting everyone.

Questions for reflection

1. Think about a job you've had. What did you learn from it? How did the job change you, helping you to become more than what you were before performing the job?

2. Do you receive just compensation for your labor, allowing you to meet all of your short-term and long-term financial obligations? Is your pay appropriate to the skills required, the competitive conditions, and the long-term sustainability of your employer? How was your rate of pay determined?

3. Think about an employer with which you are familiar. Does that employer make sure that all the rights of its employees are met? How about the right to work, the right to rest, the right to a safe working environment, and the right to form associations?

4. Do minimum-wage laws help or hinder a firm's efforts to provide just compensation to its employees? What would be the effect on wages if all minimum-wage laws were repealed?

5. Do you have a voice in the design of the job that you currently perform? How can your employer help you to reach your full potential more effectively?

Chapter 6

Integrity-Infused Customer Relationships

Every man has by nature the right to possess property as his own.

—Pope Leo XIII, *Rerum Novarum*, no. 6

Without customers, you really don't have a business. People evaluate the options available to them, make a selection, and then patronize your firm because you offer what they like. That's when they become customers.

When the products and services provided by your firm continue to perform as expected over time, customers keep coming back to buy more and become brand loyal. In this chapter, we'll discuss the right ways to develop good customer relationships and develop brand loyalty over the long haul. But we'll begin with an unusual topic. We'll start with a discussion of the importance of personal property.

Why is private-property ownership so important?

Imagine living in a society that was organized so that you didn't have to worry about the ownership or maintenance of anything. The house you lived in, the car you drove, and the place where you worked would all be owned and operated by the state. If there were a leak in the house plumbing, or your car needed new tires, or the office building needed paint, you wouldn't have to do anything, because it would be the state's responsibility to fix it. And you wouldn't have to worry about making mortgage payments or car payments! Owning nothing, you'd have no responsibilities and none of the headaches of ownership. You'd be free at last, right?

Wrong. This is the false promise of socialism. If you don't own anything, you have no independence from the entity that provides you with your daily needs. That entity, the state in this example, can manipulate you as a puppeteer operates a puppet. When your strings are pulled, you must comply with the puppeteer's every command or risk the loss of use of the house, car, or place of work. Lack of ownership firmly ties you to the wishes of the state. If the state wants you to do a certain job, marry a certain person, think a certain thought, or worship in a certain way, you will respond appropriately or suffer the sanctions that the state imposes. Private property ownership insulates the individual from this possibility. Pope Paul VI expressed it this way: "Private property ... confers on everyone a sphere wholly necessary for the autonomy of the person and the family, and it should be regarded as an extension of human freedom."[87] The right to property ownership is based on the subsidiarity principle.

Property ownership provides a buffer between you and those in power positions, and this protects your personal independence. In fact, without private-property ownership, you could not be truly free. Should a power figure such as your boss require you to do something that is contrary to your values, you can quit, sell your property, and live off the proceeds until you find another

---

[87] *Gaudium et Spes*, no. 71.

job. But if you don't own any property, you have no independence and must do the thing required or likely lose your job. Ownership provides an assurance of freedom and dignity that empowers individuals. It gives all of us the opportunity to exercise our free will and make meaningful decisions.

I learned this truth firsthand when a previous boss called me into his office and said, "Terminate Baker."

I couldn't believe my ears. William Baker worked for me as director of new product development. He was a brilliant engineer, a hard worker, and very effective in his job. I said, "You want me to fire Baker? What did he do?"

"It's not that he did anything," the boss replied. "He just stinks! He constantly smells like tobacco smoke, and I can't stand it any longer."

Baker was a heavy smoker. He had tried to quit several times, but nothing he tried worked. True, his clothes did carry a tobacco odor, but that didn't bother me as it bothered the boss. Baker was a good worker.

"But, boss, we can't fire someone just for smoking," I explained. "Baker's always careful to take his smoke breaks outdoors, and he doesn't violate any company rules."

The boss leaned over the table and growled, "Then invent something! I want him gone tomorrow. And if you can't fire him, I'll put someone in your job who can."

This whole situation seemed like a bad dream. To "invent" a reason to fire someone was clearly unethical. Other dubious directives that the boss had made over the course of our brief reporting relationship came to mind, and I realized that he was leading me down a path of escalating commitment. If I didn't say no to this one, he would require me to do something even more unethical the next time. It would be like making a pact with the devil. Fortunately, I had put some money away for a rainy day. If I refused to do what my conscience told me was wrong and lost my job as a result, I had enough private assets to feed, clothe, and house my family until I found another job. This gave me the freedom to do the right thing. After several more meetings with the boss, I was able to save Baker's job. But I also realized that I no longer could trust this boss, so I resigned from the company.

Often, those who hear this story tell me they can't believe what I'm saying is true. Certainly, the boss couldn't have been so insensitive! But after further discussion and personal reflection, these listeners will acknowledge that a similar situation occurred to them. It may not have involved firing someone, but it involved doing something that was unethical, and the consequence of failure to comply was loss of position and income. Unfortunately, there are people in this world who behave unethically, and part of our responsibility is to help them see that there is another way to address the problem, an ethical way.

There's another advantage to private-property ownership. In addition to giving you something to live on, private property also gives you control of your immediate surroundings and teaches you responsibility. I remember visiting Monterrey, Mexico, in the 1990s and being surprised to see so much trash, graffiti, and damage to property along the highway. I asked my host what was going on, and he explained that in Mexico, only a very small percentage of the population had any experience in owning something. It was a poor country. Without that experience, many in the population had not learned the responsibilities of ownership or the idea of respect for what someone else owns. Consequently, the majority of the population had no motivation to treat any property—private or public—with respect. In my subsequent travels to foreign nations, I've noticed that where property ownership is low, there's an inevitable lack of respect for property, and a corresponding lack of dignity expressed for the people. The two go together.

Business is a noble profession. Businesses engage in the great enterprise of making property available to everyone, so that all have the true freedom that ownership brings. By creating products of value, pricing them affordably, and distributing them widely, businesses help people live more fulfilling lives. This is an awesome responsibility.

Are some forms of private ownership better than others?

Private property usually refers to real property, such as land and houses; personal property, such as furniture, clothing, jewelry, art, writings, or household goods; and financial assets, such as stocks, bonds, precious metals, and cash. Businesses are involved in producing, selling, or distributing all forms of private property.

All personal property is not equal in value, however. A device with multiple uses has more value than one that can do only one thing, and something that helps its owner do good things has more value than something that does evil. Accordingly, if businesses wish to do good, they should produce products that help customers do good things. Products that are detrimental to human well-being, such as nontherapeutic drugs, pornography, gambling, violent video games, and abortion products, do not meet authentic human needs. These products bring misery, not happiness, and should not be offered.

Please pay careful attention to the following: *Market forces are not adequate to determine what should be produced.* To those of us who champion the free-enterprise system and have long extolled its virtues, this is difficult to swallow. But read what St. John Paul II had to say about the limitation of markets:

> There are collective and qualitative needs which cannot be satisfied by market mechanisms. There are important human needs which escape its logic. There are goods which by their nature cannot and must not be bought and sold. Certainly the mechanisms of the market offer secure advantages; they help to utilize resources better; they promote the exchange of products; above all they give central place to the person's desires and preferences.... Nevertheless, these mechanisms carry the risk of an idolatry of the market, an idolatry which ignores the existence of goods which by their nature are not and cannot be commodities.[88]

The logic of the market is based upon the aggregation of the needs of individual consumers as viewed by individual producers. All market inputs are valued, whether they are legitimate or not, and thus, authentic societal-level needs can get drowned out by the magnitude and variety of other individual concerns. For instance, I might believe that the quality of our environment should be protected, but when I make a purchase decision for a routine product such as toothpaste, environmental considerations take a backseat to other considerations, such as cavity-fighting effectiveness, taste, price, color, purity, packaging, and brand image. Lower-priority concerns tend to be overwhelmed by higher-priority concerns, and something as important as environmental impact can be made invisible.

[88] John Paul II, *Centesimus Annus*, no. 40.

To the producer, it would seem that the market is demanding certain important product attributes but has little concern for the greenness of the product. That producer might then make sure that his product delivers well on all the voiced product attributes, but at the same time he might ignore sustainability issues. This is the result of an idolatry of market, of placing too much authority in the way things turn out. The producer's defense is always "The market made me do it." But this approach violates the solidarity principle. Producers should protect the consumer from their own inattention and provide "good" products even when the market is not requesting them.

Metaphysics identifies four qualities of God that people appreciate and attempt to find in their daily lives: unity, truth, beauty, and goodness. Products that reflect these qualities help individuals rise above the daily grind and remind them of their ultimate destiny.

Unity is the opposite of division, and products that help heal division and enable people to come together are desirable. Michelob is on target with their tag line, "When good friends gather." *Truth* implies that products, advertising, operating instructions, and company policies are more effective when they are honest, consistent, and readily intelligible. The overuse of legalese and small-print notifications in pharmaceutical advertising, although motivated by truth, is confusing and the opposite of what truth requires. *Goodness* means that consumers appreciate what helps them achieve good ends and improves their lives. Think of Campbell soups and "M'm! M'm! Good!" *Beauty* suggests symmetry and order that results in the purchaser's delight. Good design sells. Businesses with integrity will logically develop offerings that incorporate one or more of these qualities. Producing goods that meet all the perceived needs of consumers at a competitive price is sometimes very difficult. Mistakes occur, and that's where regulation comes in.

What are the pros and cons of new-product regulation?

Each year more than thirty-three million injuries and twenty-four thousand deaths occur in the United States involving consumer products, and these injuries and deaths represent costs to society of roughly $700 billion each year.[89] Consumer product safety is an important public good, and the United States Congress has established several government agencies charged with regulating the design, production, and sale of these products so as to secure that safety.

The Competitive Enterprise Institute pegs the costs of regulatory compliance here in the United States as exceeding $1.3 trillion per year,[90] more than Canada's entire GDP. The combined costs of consumer harm and manufacturer compliance amount to over $2 trillion per year, or approximately 13 percent of the nation's GDP. These costs are ultimately passed on to consumers through higher prices for goods and services. Clearly, our current system of ensuring consumer product safety is a fairly expensive proposition.

[89] Tom Schroeder, *Consumer Product-Related Injuries and Deaths in the United States: Estimated Injuries Occurring in 2010 and Estimated Deaths Occurring in 2008* (Bethesda, MD: Consumer Products Safety Commission, 2012), pp. 1–13.

[90] Clyde Wayne Crews Jr., *Ten Thousand Commandments: An Annual Snapshot of the Federal Regulatory State* (Washington, DC: Competitive Enterprise Institute, 2016), https://cei.org/.

Integrity implies that regulatory agencies should follow the principles of subsidiarity and solidarity in carrying out their responsibilities. Subsidiarity is the principle that suggests that a national government entity should not take control over activities and responsibilities that can ordinarily be done at the local or subsidiary level.

A good example of this is the determination of safety standards. In many cases, trade associations can be the driving force in gathering safety information from producers and in creating safety standards for industry products. When a federal agency takes control of the standard-setting process, each individual producer may feel less "ownership" in the resulting standard and have less interest in ensuring that the firm's products go beyond the minimum imposed by that standard.[91] Federal control without sufficient local involvement can set up an "us versus them" mentality and encourage counterfeit acceptance—a potentially dangerous condition that can result in product recall down the road.

Solidarity is the principle that fairness should be tempered with compassion, so that the most vulnerable entities are protected from onerous regulation. For instance, even though the recalls that prompted the Consumer Product Safety Improvement Act in 2008 were related to children's toys, Congress chose to add regulations covering the certification testing of shoes, clothing, personal-care products, jewelry, educational materials, books, ATVs, and video games. A mandated quick phase-in of the new regulations caught many firms by surprise, and these firms lost millions of dollars because they had to purge

---

[91] Armin Falk and Michael Kosfeld, "The Hidden Costs of Control," *American Economic Review* 96, no. 5 (2006): 1611–1630.

inventories of suspect product, acquire expensive testing equipment to make certification tests, and turn away customers until the required certifications could be produced.

Some small businesses became unprofitable and struggled, a seeming violation of the solidarity principle. Small publishers of children's books were especially hurt, as the new law required that expensive tests be conducted to certify the level of lead in ink used to print books intended for children aged twelve or under. The same regulations required banning the sale of youth ATVs and motorcycles due to lead content in the battery terminals and valve stems.[92] Banning books, ATVs, and motorcycles out of a concern that children might contract lead poisoning by chewing on pages, battery cables, and valve stems seems to go well beyond normal limits. These actions can unfairly penalize the smaller, more vulnerable producers in these product categories.

Product safety regulation in the United States is an expensive and growing enterprise, with federal agencies controlling the safety of just about every product that a consumer can purchase. Unfortunately, regulations rarely come with sunset provisions, so once they've been enacted, firms must be aware of their existence and comply. These regulations serve to protect consumers from hazardous products, but at the same time, they represent increasing costs for firms, which must organize their business for compliance and likely expand their payroll by hiring additional help. Often these costs of compliance fall disproportionally on smaller firms.[93]

---

[92] Consumer Products Safety Commission, Consumer Product Safety Improvement Act, August 14, 2008, http://www.cpsc.gov/businfo/cpsa.pdf.

[93] W. Mark Crain (2005), *The Impact of Regulatory Costs on Small Firms* (report prepared for the Small Business Administration,

What principles should drive advertising?

My dad was fond of saying, "In advertising, you need to say what you mean, and mean what you say." That bit of advice under-scores honesty and integrity.

Integrity requires that advertising help people grow in an un-derstanding of what is unifying, true, good, and beautiful. Adver-tisers are morally responsible for what they seek to move people to do,[94] so if your firm's advertising encourages consumers to cul-tivate a lavish lifestyle or otherwise do something wrong, you are presenting a destructive vision of people and society. This can corrupt culture and undermine the cultural values we hold dear.

Integrity demands that the use of manipulative, exploitive, and corruptive methods of persuasion should be avoided. Advertising that is deceptive, whether by what it says, by what it implies, or by what it fails to say, should not be used. Further, advertising ap-peals should be consistent with the intended product benefits. All too often, sexuality is used as the principle promotional appeal, even when the product being advertised has little connection to beauty or sensuality. When consumers are constantly bombarded with sexual advertising, they begin to place a higher priority on sexuality than moderation demands. This harms society.

The adage in advertising is to "sell the sizzle, not the steak," and many advertisers believe that sex is the sizzle that will help their product move. But this is wrongheaded.

One of my clients developed a low-priced home whirlpool bath and asked me for assistance in promoting it. An analysis

---

Office of Advocacy, Contract No. SBHQ-03-M-0522, September 2005), http://www.sba.gov/advo/research/rs264tot.pdf.

[94] Pontifical Council for Social Communications, *Ethics in Advertis-ing*, February 22, 1997, www.vatican.va/.

of the promotional materials of key competitors demonstrated an overuse of sex appeal in brochures and advertisements, with many product visuals including nude models whose nudity was shielded by strategically placed soap bubbles. Competitors seemed to be saying that if you buy their whirlpool bath, you will look sexier.

A further study of the whirlpool market found that a growing consumer motivation to purchase a whirlpool bath was related to the health benefits it provides. That was an element that was not featured in any of the competitors' advertising. Consequently, I proposed a promotional campaign featuring Olympic athletes extolling the health and physical performance benefits of the deep hydrotherapy message that the client's whirlpool provided.

Unfortunately, the client didn't go for my recommendation. He was set on adopting the nude-model approach. But when he found out the costs of hiring professional beauty models, he invited some of the office staff to earn extra money by posing with the product. On the night of the shoot, the young women decided they wouldn't trust the soap bubbles to protect their modesty, so he agreed to let them wear bathing suits. Now, if any of those women are reading this, please don't be offended. You looked beautiful in your bathing suits, but the effect wasn't quite the same as with nude professional models.

Because my stubborn client wanted to go with sex appeal, and then failed to execute that strategy appropriately, the advertising failed to convey the product's key competitive advantages. After twelve months of lackluster sales, he pulled it off the market. It became one more failed new product killed by ineffective advertising. Had he used the Olympic-athlete approach, the product would have been successful.

Chipotle Mexican Grill is an example of a firm that executes a superior promotion strategy. They've constructed their promotional communications around the phrase "food integrity," which they define as "serving the very best sustainably raised food possible with an eye to great taste, great nutrition, and great value." The company's website suggests that they employ organically grown local produce and meat from animals raised without synthetic hormones. When the company was not able to obtain enough pork that met these standards, they temporarily deleted pork from the menu in some of their restaurants rather than substitute lower-quality product.

What is consumerism?

Personal property is necessary for human freedom and happiness, but there is a danger that consumers allow their natural tendency for acquisition to become outsized and dominate their lives. Consumerism is the mentality that defines success as having goods rather than being good, and that values possessions over moral character. It regards life as a striving for goods rather than a striving for goodness. Because of this disordered desire to consume more than what is necessary, Pope Francis condemns consumerism: "Since the market tends to promote extreme consumerism in an effort to sell its products, people can easily get caught up in a whirlwind of needless buying and spending."[95] This isn't beneficial for the person, and it isn't beneficial for society.

But we live in a free-enterprise society. Isn't Pope Francis overreacting a little in his condemnation of consumerism? I don't

---

[95] Francis, Encyclical *Laudato Si'*, May 24, 2015, no. 203.

think so. The evils of consumerism have long been recognized.[96] Consumerism leads people to covet what their neighbors have, to seek possessions at the expense of virtue, and to focus on immediate gratification and frivolous pleasures instead of the long-term and the truly valuable.

Think about what happens on Black Friday, the day after Thanksgiving. We all know friends and family members who head out in the middle of the night so as to arrive at a retailer's store before the rest of the crowd, in hopes of buying items at a big discount. Consumerism is neither unique to the West nor directly related to affluence. Romania and Ukraine rank as high in consumerism as the United States and New Zealand. And it afflicts people at all socioeconomic levels. In fact, impoverished youth are often more consumeristic than their wealthier counterparts. Consumerism is dangerous because it distracts us from what is really worth striving for.

Consumerism trains us to think of products as the solution to all our problems, and to think about only problems that advertised products might be able to solve. So, how can we resist this consumption disease?

Practice of the cardinal virtues offers us an antidote. The cardinal virtues enable us to engage in business and buy products without compromising human development and happiness. As discussed previously, the four cardinal virtues are habits that enable us to act well in four aspects of life: moderation regarding pleasure, courage regarding pain, justice regarding people, and prudence regarding truth and goodness.

---

[96] See, for example, St. Thomas Aquinas, *Summa Theologiae*, I-II, Q. 2, art. 1, ad. 1; Jean-Jacques Rousseau, *Discourse on the Origin of Inequity*, pt. 2; and Henry David Thoreau, *Walden*, chap. 1.

REI's Black Friday Policy

The outdoor-products retailer REI made a rather provocative announcement. They won't open their doors on Black Friday but instead encourage employees and customers to take the day off to enjoy the great outdoors. How can any retailer shut down on what has become one of the busiest shopping days of the year?

REI's Black Friday closing responds favorably to the principle of solidarity. Solidarity requires that businesses shouldn't provide everything that buyers think they want, especially if what they think they want can cause potential harm. Businesses need to keep an eye on solidarity and sell in a manner that helps customers create lifestyles of beauty, goodness, and communion with others.

"We think that Black Friday has gotten out of hand," said Jerry Stritzke, REI's CEO. Holding a one-day retail event that seems to encourage pushing and shoving, bad behavior, and consumption for the sake of consumerism is not beneficial to most customers. It's better to do what REI has done: encourage good behavior, promote enjoyment of the outdoors, and help people seek to develop their body, mind, and spirit.

There's something inconsistent with the idea that Americans spend a Thursday holiday giving thanks for all that God has given them, and then spend the following day intensely competing to acquire more. REI's promotion of an alternate approach is likely to resonate with their customers.

"This business centers on the outdoors," explained Stritzke. "We can do something like close our doors on Black Friday, and we'll have the membership that'll think that's cool."*

> *John Kell, "Why REI Is Opting Out of Black Friday Again This Year," *Fortune*, October 24, 2016, http://fortune.com/.

Moderation allows consumers to enjoy pleasures without harm to themselves, their loved ones, or their neighbors. Immoderate persons, by contrast, are slaves to their passions, which grow beyond all measure.

Moderation is not only a certain strength to master our desires; it also helps us recognize the seductive quality of consumerism and find satisfaction in becoming good rather than acquiring things. The consumerist mind-set values quantity, novelty, and present enjoyment over quality, reliability, and future enjoyment. Seeking a "good deal" becomes more important than buying products that meet a real need.

We live in a media-saturated environment that delivers hundreds of advertising messages each day. The virtue of moderation can help keep consumers from excess and help limit how far they can proceed in acting on their desires. And businesses can apply the virtue of moderation to promote products in a realistic context and not glamorize exclusive or excessive lifestyles. For instance, the men's clothing retailer Jos. A. Bank frequently runs "buy one, get two free" promotions, but does everyone really need three new suits at once? A promotion that offers a discount on one ensemble (suit, shirt, and tie) might reflect moderation but still create effective business.

The virtue of courage can help consumers resist overly persuasive sales techniques and refrain from purchasing products and services they don't need or can't afford. And businesses can apply courage, too, by refraining from manipulating consumers to buy mediocre products, and instead develop products with real advantages that appeal to customers and help them flourish.

The virtue of justice can be applied to control the consumerist tendency to seek advantage at the expense of others. And for businesses, the Golden Rule applies. Those who market products are also consumers of other products, so everyone has a personal stake in how consumers are treated. How do we want to be treated? Not by having our buttons pushed, but by appealing to our sense of the good. One such company is Rosa's Fresh Pizza (see "Integrity at Rosa's Fresh Pizza").

The virtue of prudence helps cut through the confusion of consumerism by clarifying whether something is really a problem, and if so, whether a product purchase could solve it now or later. A prudent person might continue to use or repair a product that does not have as many features as the newest version. The imprudent person chooses the transitory over the enduring. Companies can minimize the practice of planned obsolescence and develop products that will provide long-term value.

For example, the iPod is essentially a disposable product because its design makes it impossible to change the rechargeable battery. The rationale, no doubt, is that consumers will want an up-to-date iPod rather than repair an outmoded one. But this

Integrity at Rosa's Fresh Pizza

"Helping the community, one slice at a time" is the advertising slogan of Rosa's Fresh Pizza, founded by a young entrepreneur named Mason Wartman, who left Wall Street at the age of twenty-five to open a dollar-a-slice pizzeria in Philadelphia.

If you walk into his store, you will immediately notice that the walls are lined with colorful Post-it notes, usually with a word of encouragement from the customers who placed them there. Each note can be redeemed for a free slice of pizza by anyone who is hungry and can't afford to buy one.

How did this begin? One customer brought the Italian tradition of "suspended coffees" into the pizzeria by walking in and asking if he could buy a slice for someone who couldn't afford one. Mason quickly accepted the donation to reserve the "suspended pizza." Soon the word spread, and within ten months, Rosa's Fresh Pizza had served nine thousand slices to people who couldn't afford to buy a meal.

"This program works because it allows our customers a way to respect the dignity of those who are poor and express solidarity with them," Mason explained. "These are important values that our customers hold dear."

In the American marketplace, Rosa's "suspended pizza" program is something of a serendipitous anomaly, at least so far. But it is easily replicable by other types of business, and it is likely that other forward-thinking business owners will adopt similar "suspended product" promotions. Such actions have the potential not just to affect one city block but to transform the whole marketplace, local and global, with seeds of innovation and entrepreneurship all aimed at realizing the common good.*

*This story is based on information provided by Cabrini Pak of the Busch School of Business and Economics at the Catholic University of America.

might change if inexpensively priced replacement parts were available. When companies produce items with durable value in mind, consumers will come to associate a brand with stability and reliance.

Virtuous producers recognize that there is a proper and ethical way to run a business, and this is the surest path to success. They understand, too, that businesspeople are not simply agents of the business but human beings whose own character is at stake in their activities. To focus on authentic human good, businesses can display their products as accessories to a good life, rather than the substance of that life.

So, what's the bottom line? How can businesses and consumers solve the problem of consumerism? When consumers and business managers both practice virtue, the bad effects of consumerism are reduced, and all of society benefits. Instead of the unbridled appetites for more, the desire for one's own advantage at the expense of others, the consideration of only easy solutions to life's problems, or the attempt to rest in passing pleasure, the cardinal virtues open up another possibility. And it's one that both consumers and producers can appreciate and promote.

Questions for reflection

1. Imagine that you woke up one day to find that your country had confiscated all private-property ownership rights and replaced them with subsidies based on need, as determined by the state. Instead of a home and investment portfolio, you now had a government check. What would that do to your freedom? Can government payments ever replace individual ownership and savings?

2. Can free markets really make moral determinations? What are the potential limitations to markets that business leaders can correct by applying integrity in decision-making?

3. Do you know anyone who seems to be bitten by the consumerism bug? What are the symptoms you observe? What can you do to help "cure" that person?

4. Who should determine which products should be marketed and sold? Can you identify any products that should never be produced? Whose job is it to police this?

5. Are you loyal to any one brand? Which one? What is it about their offering that makes you continue to want to buy it? Can you relate this to integrity?

Chapter 7

Integrity, Regulation, and Society

You may fool all of the people some of the time; you
may even fool some of the people all of the time; but
you can't fool all of the people all of the time.

—Attributed to Abraham Lincoln

I was in Bern, Switzerland, meeting with our new Swiss business partner when I got a message from the managing director of an Austrian company who wanted to meet me for lunch. His company was the dominant player in our type of products for both Austria and Switzerland, and he obviously had gotten word that my company was making plans to launch in Switzerland. We had a cordial lunch at a nice restaurant, and as the plates were being cleared, he leaned forward, drew an imaginary line on the table cloth, and clenched his fist. He looked me square in the eyes and said in excellent English, "Switzerland is our market. If your company persists in developing plans to sell your products here, it won't go well for you."

Apparently, he had watched some American cowboy movies and presumed that American businesses back off only when threatened. To me, it seemed as if we had just been transported to a Wild West saloon and I had just been told to get out of town on the noon train! So I pulled my Stetson lower on my brow and fingered my Colt 45. (Just kidding!) I asked, "In what way won't it go well?"

"Look, if you stay away from our Swiss market, we'll stay away from your Italian market and we'll both be happy," he replied. "But if you come into Switzerland," he continued, "we'll come after you in Italy with low prices and you'll lose money—lots of money trying to compete. We're local. We have a huge cost advantage."

The core principles of integrity fit well with an American-style spirit of enterprise. When markets are open and have minimal entry barriers, all of society benefits through a wider assortment of products and lower prices. Firms that have a better idea of how to serve customers can enter the market and prove themselves. Consumers choose by patronizing the brands they like best. Firms that get beat by a better brand have the opportunity to refine their offering and come back with a new offer. The result is continuing innovation and a vibrant market.

That's why the proposal by the Austrian managing director was so offensive. Sure, dividing the market could result in more profits for both companies short-term, but consumers would be denied the opportunity to choose, and the firms themselves would be denied the opportunity to learn consumer preferences in the crucible of a fair and competitive market. Consequently, in my reply, I got to demonstrate a little bravado. I explained that we were confident that our products could compete throughout Europe, and that my company was not afraid of competition. Our intention was to become a global brand, and that meant offering our products in every market, including Switzerland.

Laws are necessary to keep markets fair and competitive. In previous chapters, we examined the ethical treatment of employees and customers. In this chapter, we will look at how laws and regulation impact the conduct of business.

Federal, state, and local governments in the United States have implemented laws and regulations intended to protect businesses, workers, consumers, and the environment. How many laws are there? Nobody knows. According to a 2011 article in the *Wall Street Journal*, the task of counting the number of laws has bedeviled lawyers, academics, and government officials.[97] An attempt to count the number of laws in the Federal Criminal Code took two years and failed to reach a conclusive count. With multiple laws covering thousands of possible crimes, researchers often have had difficulty agreeing whether individual laws are individually distinct or duplicates of other laws.

My cousin served for many years as an environmental-law specialist. I asked him how many laws there were that protected the environment. He merely nodded toward two huge bookshelves loaded top to bottom with thick law books, and said in his Texas drawl, "Don't know, but there are the more important ones."

The sheer number of laws of all types that are on the books makes it more challenging for businessmen to know the laws and observe them. Yet this is an important undertaking. Ignorance of the law is no excuse.

How do laws provide an ethical minimum?

History has revealed that if unregulated by government, some businesses will utilize economic and political power to take advantage of those in weaker positions. An analysis of the industrial

[97] Gary Fields and John R. Emshwiller, "Many Failed Efforts to Count Nation's Federal Crime Laws," *Wall Street Journal*, July 23, 2011.

revolution of the late 1800s in the United States demonstrates this point. A number of unethical businessmen, including John Astor, Andrew Carnegie, Jay Gould, J. P. Morgan, John D. Rockefeller, Cornelius Vanderbilt, and others, were derogatorily called "robber barons" because they conspired to create monopolies, dominate markets, and charge monopolistic prices.[98] Children were sometimes utilized as a cheap labor source, and dangerous and unhealthy working conditions were commonplace. Workers were viewed as merely expendable objects to be paid low wages, overworked, and then fired if they became injured and could no longer work.

This exploitation of labor existed for several decades, but the public outcry against the monopoly owners eventually became so widespread that legislatures began passing laws to provide employee protections. To prevent employers from taking unfair advantage, legislatures enacted laws to provide a threshold level of ethical treatment that all must meet. Certainly, companies could exceed those threshold levels. In fact, integrity demands that firms make sure that everything they do is in the proper proportion: that human dignity is respected, that solidarity and subsidiarity is practiced, and that the common good is achieved. Firms should not use the legal threshold level as the most they will do — it's only the minimum requirement.

Legislatures recognized that regulation was necessary to protect the rights and well-being of the weaker members of society, and eventually, they even extended protection to businesses. This new protection leveled the playing field to promote free

---

[98] Edward J. Renehan, *Dark Genius of Wall Street: The Misunderstood Life of Jay Gould, King of the Robber Barons* (New York: Basic Books, 2006).

Tylenol and the Ethics of FDA Regulation

Tylenol was a preferred over-the-counter (OTC) pain-killer even before the 1982 "Tylenol Scare," when seven Chicago-area residents died from tampered Extra Strength Tylenol products that had been laced with cyanide. Within a week, McNeil Laboratories and its parent company, Johnson and Johnson, pulled thirty-one million bottles of Tylenol tablets back from retailers, making it one of the first and most successful major recalls in American history.

Its fast action and effective public relations during the recall earned the company accolades and preserved the good brand name of the product for its manufacturer. The great scare led to new safety initiatives, including tamper-proof lids and gelcaps. As a result, the Tylenol brand prospered, remained a top seller, and today controls about 35 percent of the painkiller market in North America.

But sometimes a company can lose its ethical moorings, especially when a government agency such as the Food and Drug Administration (FDA) advocates a "do nothing" approach.

McNeil offered two versions of Tylenol for youngsters: Children's Tylenol, intended for children up to eleven years old, and Infant's Tylenol, which was three times stronger, for children who didn't like to take medication. Consistent with FDA regulations, neither medication provided dosage instructions for children who were under two years old. Instead, the labels of both products simply said, "Call your doctor" to obtain dosage information. The FDA's rationale was that because overdosing is such a big problem, it was better for doctors to get involved in determining how much should be given to babies rather than allowing parents to make the decision.

Unfortunately, Tylenol is acetaminophen, a product that can be lethal when overdosed. It is estimated that 150 people die from acetaminophen overdose each year, and many are under two years old when they die. Parents can't reach their doctor for advice and end up giving their sick child too much medication. Despite McNeil's frequent requests to allow printed dosage recommendations that provide parents with dosage for all ages of children, the FDA refused to grant approval. McNeil could have pulled the product from the market at any time, but they chose to do nothing. After all, they were following FDA rules to the letter.

Finally, in 2011, after eight years of lobbying the FDA and an unknown number of deaths, McNeil pulled the triple-strength version of Infant Tylenol from the market. A company that had won accolades for responding after just seven people died in 1982 failed to respond in this second case until twenty-nine years later, after many more deaths had occurred.*

*T. Christian Miller and Jeff Gerth, "Dose of Confusion," *ProPublica*, September 20, 2013, https://www.propublica.org.

and open competition. Most of these laws and ancillary regulations have supported the principles of human dignity, solidarity, subsidiarity, and the common good and have served to make the world a better place. Unfortunately, occasionally, laws are passed that have unjust elements in them.

What should we do when a law is unjust?

Everyone should conduct his or her affairs in accord with the good laws duly passed by our government. A good law is defined as one that is consistent with the natural law and therefore does not require a person or business to lie, cheat, steal, kill, or do damage to someone's marriage. Members of society should obey good laws even though there might be a personal disagreement about the purpose or wisdom of the law itself. For instance, there are federal and state laws that require citizens to pay income taxes. As taxpayers, sometimes we may not agree with the fairness of the tax laws or how the government spends collected tax revenues, but ethically speaking, we still should obey.

Bad laws occur because the legislative process is imperfect. Often unjust means are used to achieve just ends. But the ends can never be used to justify unethical means, as this creates a bad law. We can't condone lying or stealing or killing just because we are trying to achieve an end that is good. Consequently, it is ethically correct to resist or even disobey a bad law.

One example of bad law is the Health and Human Service's contraception mandate. This law requires that all health-insurance plans include coverage for abortion-inducing drugs, sterilization procedures, and contraceptives. The mandate allows no exceptions for church-affiliated schools, hospitals, and charities whose religious principles conflict with the mandate. This makes it a bad law because it forces individuals to pay for abortion coverage even if that individual is convinced that abortion is the killing of human life. This is a law intending to secure a good (a women's control over her own situation), but achieving it by bringing about evil (the killing of an innocent human life). One hundred ten businesses have joined lawsuits to fight this legislation. All persons have a responsibility to work toward the repeal of bad laws, no matter whether they impact us or not.

But some may balk at that idea. Business organizations don't vote; that's the responsibility of citizens. Shouldn't businesses just keep quiet and obey the laws that are passed without comment? No. Integrity demands that business organizations have a responsibility to society to make sure that all laws provide a moral minimum that is fair and just. This is a key component of any business's responsibility to society.

Do businesses have a responsibility to society?

Do you remember the story about high finance that Jesus told His followers in Matthew 25:14–30? In the story, an investor delegates the management of his accumulated wealth to three financial consultants. He gives $5 million to the first consultant, $2 million to the second, and $1 million to the third. At the end of the year, he asks for an accounting. Two of the consultants achieve 100 percent returns by trading in the equity markets, but the third consultant places the money in non-interest-bearing government securities and earns nothing. The investor is delighted with the performance of the first two but severely criticizes the third. Okay, this is an updated translation of the story!

The meaning of the parable extends far beyond financial investments. Each of us as individuals, and each of the businesses we represent, have been given a variety of resources, and we are expected to employ those resources so that they accomplish good things. If we don't make that happen, we are misusing the resources we've been given.

Like the three consultants, we do not all have the same amount of investment funds available, but the return that the investor expects from us is commensurate with the resources that the investor has placed at our disposal. When we realize that God is the investor, we see that the resources we've been given are immense. They include our money and property, of course, but they also extend to our time, skills, abilities, connections, education, and experience. The severe consequences to the unproductive consultant, far beyond anything triggered by mere business mediocrity, tell us that we are to invest our lives, not to waste them. Those who possess great resources have great responsibilities.

Christianity teaches that all of creation is a gift from God and mankind is the appointed steward responsible for seeing to it that the benefits of this creation are made available to everyone.[99] This fundamental principle, that all creation is ultimately God's, and therefore belongs to all God's creatures, is known as the *universal destination of material goods*. Those whom God provides with an abundance of material goods are required to invest them so that they pay off for everyone, especially the poorest of the poor. This obligation is sometimes referred to as our *social mortgage*,[100] or *the preferential option for the poor*.[101] The idea stems from the principles of common good and solidarity.

---

[99] *Gaudium et Spes*, no. 26.

[100] John Paul II, Encyclical *Sollicitudo Rei Socialis*, December 30, 1987, no. 42.

[101] John Paul II, *Centesimus Annus*, no. 57.

The solidarity principle requires that good team members are always available to assist those members who are in great difficulty. Economic activity has the potential to raise everyone who participates, so it is a tragedy when someone is excluded from participation. Pope Francis complains that when systems are structured to favor competition and the survival of the fittest, the powerful feed upon the powerless. Consequently, many people find themselves excluded, without work, without possibilities, and without means of escape.[102] Integrity requires that businesses address the needs of those who are not able to participate in the economic system.

It is instructive at this point to review current understandings of corporate social responsibility (CSR), both in the literature and in business practice. Such an understanding has increased in importance as a result of rising public concerns regarding consumer protection and environmentalism.

CSR begins with the idea that businesses are created to fulfill a specific need in society. Individuals come together to form businesses because of the belief that a group of individuals, acting together, can fulfill society's need better, more completely, or more efficiently than individuals acting alone.[103] Consequently, businesses are perceived to have obligations to society, and these obligations are called *corporate social responsibility*.[104]

The literature describes at least five distinct models of CSR: (1) the profit maximization, (2) the moral minimum, (3) the

---

[102] Francis, Apostolic Exhortation *Evangelii Gaudium*, November 24, 2013, no. 53.

[103] Debbie Thorne McAlister, O. C. Ferrell, and Linda Ferrell, *Business and Society: A Strategic Approach to Social Responsibility* (Boston: Houghton Mifflin, 2005), chap. 1.

[104] Ibid.

marketing concept, (4) the stakeholder concept, and (5) the societal concept. All these models require that businesses, first and foremost, obey the law.

The *profit-maximization* model posits that businesses serve society best by making decisions and implementing actions that maximize the return on invested capital.[105] This model dominated corporate practice from the industrial revolution until the consumer revolution of the 1960s. It is a strictly legalistic view that looks to the articles of incorporation of the business and concludes that because no responsibility to entities other than the shareholder is defined, there is no such responsibility. But it is a view that does not correspond to moral integrity. Business leaders need to look beyond shareholders to understand their responsibilities to society.

The *moral-minimum* model posits that in addition to generating profits and obeying laws, businesses are responsible for cleaning up their messes so that their operations leave no negative impact on society.[106] Thus, the business that strip-mines coal from the earth has the responsibility of creating parks and recreation areas where the mining took place; or the business that produces tobacco has a responsibility to pay for the medical bills of those who get sick from consuming its products. The legal system in the United States has increasingly held this viewpoint, as evidenced in the mounting precedence of court decisions since the 1960s.

---

[105] Duncan W. Reekie, "Should Firms Maximize Profits?" *Journal of Economic Affairs* 2, no. 2 (1982): 90–93.

[106] Brian Engelland and William Eshee Jr., *Ethics Essentials for Business Leaders* (Rockville Centre, NY: Sophia Omni Press, 2011), pp. 51–52.

The *marketing-concept* model asserts that businesses not only have the responsibility of generating profits, obeying laws, and cleaning up after themselves but also have an obligation to balance the needs of customers and of the organization in creating maximum value for both.[107] In fact, success in generating profits is clearly linked to how much better than its competitors a firm understands the needs of customers and marshals its resources to meet those needs. The marketing discipline endorsed this view of business in the 1970s, and it continued to dominate marketing textbooks through the 1980s.

The *stakeholder* model states that businesses exist to benefit customers as a first priority, and that in order to benefit customers in the long term, businesses must return value to all entities that have a stake in their success.[108] These entities include shareholders, who deserve a good return on their investment; employees, who deserve good wages, benefits, and working conditions; suppliers, who deserve consistent and fair opportunities to supply the business; and the community at large, which deserves a clean environment and the benefits of favorable economic growth. Much of the current literature in the marketing and management disciplines endorses this model of business.

Finally, the *societal-concept* model, also called the *business-citizenship* model,[109] expects more from business enterprises than profits, cleaning up messes, or merely benefiting those with a stake in the business. Under the societal concept model, businesses

---

[107] Philip Kotler, "A Generic Concept of Marketing," *Journal of Marketing* 36 (1972): 46–54.

[108] Anne Gregory, "Involving Stakeholders in Developing Corporate Brands: The Communication Dimension," *Journal of Marketing Management* 23, nos. 1–2 (2007): 59–73.

[109] Engelland and Eshee, *Ethics Essentials*, pp. 52–53.

have the responsibility of using their resources, capabilities, and scale to improve life across all areas of society: to help improve education, alleviate poverty, eliminate prejudice, cure misery, and a host of other humanitarian goals. [110] Advocates of this model presume that large corporations have a great potential for doing good and have an inherent moral responsibility to fulfill that potential well.

Given the fact that marketing textbooks and journals have been endorsing stakeholder and societal models for the last twenty years, one might think that America's corporations have also been adopting this enlightened understanding of corporate social responsibility and making the earth's abundance available to everyone. Ostensibly, this should include a renewed sense of responsibility to protect consumers by vetting all new product ideas thoroughly and making sure that nothing is released to the market unless it is wholesome, good, and absolutely safe.

Unfortunately, given the results of notable product recalls in the recent news, many companies may still be firmly attached to profit responsibility as their preferred view. Those that follow the profit-maximization model are likely to have a more restricted concern for the safety of the products they produce and sell than those manufacturers that follow other models of CSR. Profit-maximization firms would be concerned with safety issues only to the extent that such issues adversely impact sales levels or drive up legal costs. Moral-minimum firms would have a higher level of concern due to the real costs of rectifying any harm their products cause. Marketing-concept firms would have a higher

---

[110] Russell Abratt and Diane Sacks, "The Marketing Challenge: Towards Being Profitable and Socially Responsible," *Journal of Business Ethics* 7 (July 1988): 497–507.

level of concern due to their customer motivation. Stakeholder-model firms would have an even greater level of concern due to their multiple stakeholder motivation. And societal-concept firms would have the greatest level of concern due to their altruistic motivations.

If all firms would adhere to a genuine societal-concept understanding of their corporate social responsibility, then laws and regulations likely would be less important and the agencies they've fostered would undertake more limited (and less costly) roles. But that's not where we find ourselves today. Regulation is the norm, and it is increasing.

What obligations do we have to the environment?

There's a story about a farmer who buys some property and, over several years, clears the land of brambles and brush, reroutes the creek, builds a farmhouse and a barn, erects a picket fence, creates a pasture for horses, and plants flowers and crops. A friend visits and, seeing this well-maintained property, says, "What a beautiful place! It is truly amazing what God has wrought!"

The farmer thinks a moment, then replies, "That may be, but you should have seen this property when God was taking care of it Himself."

I tell this story because it helps dramatize the idea that humans have a role in creation. God gave us time, intelligence, talent, and resources, and expects our cooperation by tilling and looking after the garden that we call Earth (see Gen. 2:15) and maintaining its suitability as a home for all life. Today's businesses do most of the "tilling." Businesses build homes and communities, create transportation networks, develop labor-saving products, and distribute needed products that make Earth an enjoyable and supportive place to live. But in recent years, there has been a question about whether what we are doing is sustainable.

Sustainability is the latest buzzword in the world of business. It has replaced *environmental impact*, *social issues*, *cost containment*, and *social responsibility* in the corporate lexicon, and it touches on such far-ranging concerns as food supply, climate change, poverty, and human justice. According to a Coca-Cola VP, sustainability is now the top priority in business. The problem, however, is that no one seems to be able to agree on what sustainability is or how to attain it.

Recently I attended a sustainability conference that attracted corporate executives and scholars from around the world. During the opening session, a veteran United Nations specialist asked everyone to propose his or her own definition of *sustainability*. One academic scholar stated, "Sustainability is taking steps so that our planet doesn't fry in the next forty years." Then a business executive said, "Sustainability is making economic and policy decisions that our future grandchildren would appreciate."

I jumped in by saying, "Our biggest problem is that too often we take a short-term orientation when we make important decisions. Sustainability requires the opposite. Sustainability requires actions that pay off over the long term in building a more person-centered economy." I sat down thinking I had nailed the definition, but a scholar from California exclaimed, "No! Not person centered. That's too limiting. With all the species now at risk of extinction, we need to build a *being-*centered world!"

I disagree, and so does Pope Francis. In his encyclical on the environment, Pope Francis noted that many of the problems with the environment are due to a "failure to recognize the primacy of human beings."[111] We are placing too much faith in science and technology, and too little concern on its effects on the human person. We need to move more toward a person-centered economy.

Building a person-centered economy is necessary to improve family life and build communities that will help humans flourish. Only when the quality of human life improves—when we can reduce poverty, disease, hunger, and crime—will we be able to muster the political will and muscle to address the long-term survival of endangered plants and animals. We can't do everything at once. We need to prioritize, and that means first addressing the problems and concerns affecting people.

A person-centered economy recognizes the primacy of human beings and forms our decision-making so that we value the foundational integrity principles of human dignity, solidarity, subsidiarity, and the common good. These principles provide a "systematic approach for finding solutions to problems, so that discernment, judgment, and decisions will correspond to reality"[112] and overcome the present short-term bias in decision-making. They give us direction and an action agenda to improve the conditions for life on earth. The result will be improved conditions for human flourishing—and that's the ultimate sustainability.

How can integrity inform sustainability?

Much progress has been made in cleaning up the environment and reducing poverty in developing nations. But there is no denying that the environment is not as clean as it could be and poverty is still a significant problem. Pope Francis suggests that

---

[111] Francis, *Laudato Si'*, no. 90.
[112] Pontifical Council for Justice and Peace, *Compendium*, no. 9.

much more progress can and should be made, and he calls for a frank discussion on how this might be accomplished:

> The urgent challenge to protect our common home includes a concern to bring the whole human family together to seek a sustainable and integral development, for we know that things can change. The Creator does not abandon us; he never forsakes his loving plan or repents of having created us. Humanity still has the ability to work together in building our common home.[113]

Ecology is the study of the relationship between living organisms and the environment in which they develop.[114] But not all living organisms require the same environment, and when we speak about humans we need to apply a little more precision. We can do that by focusing on *integral ecology*, which Pope Francis describes as the field of study that places the human person at the center of it all.

Integral ecology incorporates understanding of social, cultural, economic, and environmental systems. After all, the analysis of environmental issues cannot be separated from the analysis of the person, the family, and the community in which humans develop. Integral ecology is directed at promoting the common good, not only for today, but for the future as well. True ecology first requires respect for human dignity.

In our zeal to protect the environment, we often shoot ourselves in the foot. Earlier in my career I witnessed such a situation.

The Environmental Protection Agency (EPA) had issued new restrictions on the amount and type of pollutants that

[113] Francis, *Laudato Si'*, no. 13.
[114] Ibid.

could be released into the atmosphere, and the plumbing-products company I worked for naturally wanted to adhere to these new standards. Polluting the environment goes against what we viewed as our social responsibility, and we wanted to do our part in making our common home a cleaner place.

We evaluated whether we could add scrubbers to our production stacks to clean the exhaust before it was released into the atmosphere, and we realized that the costs to do so would make our products uncompetitive. We asked for a delay in the implementation, or a phase-in so that we could find lower-cost technologies to clean the exhaust. Our requests for accommodations were denied. As a result, we had no choice but to close our plant and lay off the 250 workers employed there. Our customers began to buy similar products made by companies in Brazil, where the pollution laws were much less stringent.

With the implementation of these new standards, the EPA was successful in reducing the level of pollution coming from manufacturing plants in the United States. But the result was not a cleaner environment. Rather, production of plumbing products for the U.S. market was transferred to the less regulated, "dirtier" plants in foreign countries, and the total amount of pollution given off into the world's atmosphere increased. Furthermore, 250 people at our factory lost their jobs, resulting in personal hardship, family dislocation, and unemployment costs for the local community and state.

If an integral-ecology perspective were applied to this decision, the EPA would have evaluated the short-term and long-term effects of the change in rules and would likely have entertained approaches that might mitigate the adverse effects on human lives. Perhaps some sort of phase-in period would have provided the time for my company to react more effectively so that the pollution issues could be solved without employee dislocation. Then we could have protected families *and* the environment at the same time. If we keep shooting ourselves in the foot, we will run out of feet!

The earth is home to a vast biodiversity in which plants and animals exist in a symbiotic relationship. Through the process of photosynthesis, plants use solar energy to break down carbon dioxide into oxygen and carbon used for plant growth. Animals breathe air to gather oxygen and consume plants for food, giving off carbon dioxide as waste.

Obviously, this is an oversimplification, but the earth functions best when the atmosphere contains the proper balance of oxygen and carbon dioxide. Scientists tell us that when the balance is disrupted, climate change can be the unintended result. And since we want the earth to continue to be an effective home for our grandchildren and great-grandchildren, we need to maintain the balance by either reducing carbon dioxide emissions or planting more trees.

Pope Francis acknowledges that the Catholic Church does not have specialized authority or expertise regarding environmental technology. It can't provide guidance as to how we might increase the development of renewable energy while weaning ourselves off the use of fossil fuels. Nor does it have the expertise to contribute to the science of climate change. The Church does have competency on moral issues, however, and the care of our common home is an important moral issue.

Consequently, Pope Francis is urging everyone to join in the discussion in seeking solutions that move well beyond the current focus on technology development and carbon taxes. Integral ecology means examining how humans can flourish socially, culturally, economically, spiritually, and sustainably.

Solutions will come when all these factors are integrated more effectively, and business has the capability to help achieve this integration.

How does trust fit in?

All business transactions necessarily require that the parties trust each other to carry out their side of the agreement. All parties to the transactions must believe that the others will follow through and do what they promised to do. Trust is the glue that holds capitalism together. When ethics fail, trust fails. With good ethics, trust flourishes. Any discussion of ethics would be incomplete without including trust.

If business firms did not trust each other, very little business would get done. Can you imagine a world in which no business honored its contractual obligations? Because of this universal breach of trust, business would grind to a halt, and the court systems could not possibly handle all the cases. Businesses, employers, employees, customers, suppliers, creditors, debtors, and others would all be suing each other. But then, who would trust the court system to adjudicate? Or the jury to render a fair verdict? Author and motivational speaker Brian Tracy calls trust the "glue that holds relationships together." That glue is based on integrity. Without integrity, everything falls apart. Financier Warren Buffet remarked, "It takes twenty years to build a reputation and five minutes to ruin it."

Integrity builds trust, and trust supports many positive outcomes. Trust builds confidence in corporate management when it has established a pattern of ethical behavior. The customer knows he can depend on the product or service. The supplier knows he will be paid. The employee knows he will be treated fairly and equitably. Society can depend on the firm making ethically correct business decisions.

Good business relations are a direct result of a viable and trusting relationship. When disputes develop — and we know that disputes are inevitable — an environment of trust will enable the parties to move forward in an effort to resolve their dispute without litigation. Once the dispute is settled, the parties who have had a good trust relationship will have an opportunity to continue doing business together. Expensive litigation is thus avoided, and because no harsh feelings result from the dispute, the firms can continue their profitable relationship.

Trust is ordinarily not established instantly, or even quickly, between parties. It is usually nurtured over time. When trust is established, it sets the stage for long-term dealings between the parties. They know they can depend on each other. Long-term dealings enable management to look and plan beyond next quarter or next year. Long-term, effective planning allows a firm to position its resources so as take advantage of market conditions, thereby enhancing profits.

Trust reduces the cost of doing business. When more trust is placed in workers, less management oversight is needed. Less management expenses translate into a larger bottom line. Trust and honesty are like brother and sister. Trustworthy employees do not steal from the firm; therefore, theft losses to the firm are minimized. In firms whose nature of business requires teamwork, trust among teams and team members fosters efficiency.

In an environment of trust, workers are happier and more productive. Their attitudes are better, and they do their jobs better. This attitude may be passed on to suppliers, customers, and others. A company with a good ethical record for truth, honesty, integrity, and fairness forms the basic structure of capitalism.

Here, trust flourishes and permeates the company, and touches all those with whom the company deals. Customer satisfaction is enhanced. Stockholder confidence is strengthened, and the company is lauded as a good corporate citizen.

Questions for reflection

1. When might it make sense for a firm to provide employees with pay or benefits that exceed what is required by the law?
2. Can you think of a law that is unjust? Why is it unjust? What is the good that the regulatory body was hoping to achieve? How does that law go against the natural law?
3. Think about a company you know well. How would you describe the way this company defines its social responsibility? What evidence can you provide?
4. The state has a responsibility to promote economic activity and employment. How can it do so when it is also charged with regulation of the environment?

Chapter 8

Conditions that Lead to Good Decisions

While we are free to choose our actions, we are not free to choose the consequences of our actions.

—Attributed to Stephen R. Covey

In recent years, the United States witnessed an unprecedented number of ethical missteps among corporations. High-profile executives have been tried and found guilty of some significant ethical violations. These include fraud (Jeffrey Skilling and Kenneth Lay, former CEOs of Enron), larceny (Dennis Kozlowski, former CEO of Tyco), making false filings (Bernie Ebbers, former CEO of WorldCom), running a Ponzi scheme (Bernie Madoff, CEO of Madoff Investment Securities), and insider trading (Martha Stewart, CEO of Martha Stewart, Inc.). The list of firms implicated in ethical misdeeds includes such major corporations as Adelphia Communications, Arthur Andersen, Boeing, HealthSouth, Qwest, Volkswagen, and Wells Fargo.

These ethical breeches have caused shareholders to lose billions of dollars, corporations to go bankrupt, innocent employees to lose their jobs, and a trusting public to lose confidence in corporations and corporate leaders.

Force for Good

The number and severity of recent ethical breakdowns suggests that we are not dealing with just a few bad apples. Rather, ethical violations appear to be widespread at the highest levels of all types of organizations. And sadly, what we've seen in the newspaper may be only the tip of the iceberg, since many ethical lapses in America's organizations, corporations, and institutions never appear in the news media. Certainly the leaders of these companies should be able to do a lot better than this.

It is easy for us to look at ethical misconduct and dismiss those who did it as crooks or just bad people. We can easily rationalize that if we had been in their shoes, we would have acted differently and would have avoided the ethical violations that caused their downfall. Unfortunately, this attitude may be a dangerous rationalization. Yes, some were greedy and sought their own interests from the beginning. But most were basically good people and accomplished executives who tried to do the right thing. It was not for lack of good intentions that they failed.

Why did they fail? Most failed because they paid too little attention to how integrity should be a part of every decision. Without a good understanding of ethical decision-making, any of us could fall victim to the same errors.

Research suggests that the reasons for these lapses include (1) undeveloped personal moral standards, (2) ignoring one's own personal standards, (3) insufficient input from colleagues, (4) yielding to time pressures to make an incomplete or suboptimal decision, (5) failing to adhere to an organization's code of conduct, and (6) favoring one stakeholder group over others. In the following paragraphs, we'll discuss each of these reasons. Then we'll look at another reason that doesn't appear in the research, but one that I think is the most significant reason of all.

A framework for understanding ethical decision-making

A Framework for Ethical Decision-Making is offered to help organize our discussion. It's based upon the understanding that ethical decisions in business are strongly influenced by the personal ethical standards of the key decision-maker.

Other factors that influence the decision-maker are the organization's ethical culture, the time pressures involved in making and communicating decisions, performance pressures exerted by key stakeholders, and the influence of trusted colleagues and advisers. All of these play a role in determining when and how the businessperson responds in an ethical-decision situation.

Framework for Understanding Ethical Decision-Making
Adapted from Ferrell, Freedrich, and Ferrell (2005)

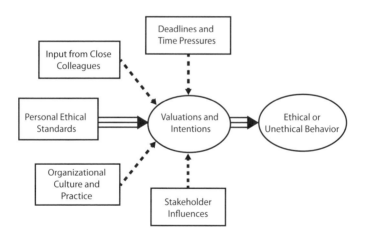

Businesspeople are constantly observing what is going on around them. They evaluate the performance of their employees, observe the reactions of key customers, and look for opportunities to enhance the performance of their organization as new challenges appear. This monitoring activity compares what is happening with what should be happening. When activities are observed that are unexpected or leading in the wrong direction, the businessperson is moved to take action that attempts to restore everything to a right condition. This process of restoration is called decision-making. When questions about rights and obligations are involved in the decision, the process is considered ethical decision-making.

Personal ethical standards

Through prior education, family environment, religious training, life experience, and job expectations, businesspeople develop a personal sense of right and wrong. This personal ethical sense influences which business conditions are dealt with and which are singled out for decision-making.

Most people learn and internalize their sense of right and wrong many years before they assume positions of responsibility. Children learn a sense of fair play, truthfulness, and respect for others that becomes ingrained and lasting through parental influences, relationships with their sibling, and early socialization.

Continued training through schooling, study, reading, and personal development helps to develop good ethical behavior by the time an adult assumes a business position. However, when the practitioner is underprepared and lacking in ethical training, the result can be *moral myopia*,[115] an inability to recognize

---

[115] Minette E. Drumwright and Patrick E. Murphy, "How Advertising Practitioners View Ethics: Moral Muteness, Moral Myopia, and Moral Imagination," *Journal of Advertising* 33, no. 2 (Summer 2004): 7–24.

moral issues that require attention. Moral myopia results in poor recognition of moral conflicts, poor decision-making ability, and poor decisions.

An executive once told me, "I know business ethics—I took a college course in it." It turns out that he had taken an undergraduate ethics course twenty years previously, and he incorrectly assumed that he knew everything he needed to know about how to manage ethically. Later we found out that this executive was leading an organization that had intentionally and systematically overbilled key customers for an extended period. Apparently, he slept through the lecture on honesty!

Obviously, one course in business ethics taken long ago may be insufficient to overcome moral myopia. Businesspeople need to continue to learn about ethics, to recognize how moral standards apply in various situations they encounter, and to grow in ethical decision-making ability throughout their careers.

Sometimes an individual divides his morality into two camps: personal and business. But St. Matthew wrote, "No one can serve two masters; for either he will hate the one and love the other, or he will be devoted to the one and despise the other. You cannot serve God and mammon" (Matt. 6:24).

Leading a divided life is one of the more serious errors of our age. Dividing the demands of one's faith from one's work contributes greatly to the damage done in our world today.[116] It places excessive confidence in material resources and worldly success. When this happens, the individual risks valuing status and fame over lasting accomplishment. That individual engages in *moral muteness*[117] by withholding his or her own good sense from input

---

[116] *Gaudium et Spes*, no. 43.
[117] Ibid.

into business-related decisions. Unfortunately, moral muteness occurs at all levels of a business organization.

A young industrial-products sales representative from the Midwest told me the following anecdote. She had been transferred to the New York sales district. During sales calls, she took meticulous notes about what was discussed and specifically wrote down what the client said so that she could take appropriate follow-up action with the home office. After developing what she thought was a good relationship with one buyer, she was surprised to hear that buyer make a statement about competitive pricing that was completely the opposite of what she had written in her notes from the previous meeting. She rechecked her notes, confirmed the discrepancy, and questioned the buyer. When he persisted, she called him on it and said, "I'm really disappointed that you lied to me! I thought we were friends."

In reply, the buyer said, "But we *are* friends. I would never lie to you as a friend. I was only lying as part of our negotiations. Certainly you understand that lying is a normal business activity!"

Unfortunately, many business leaders get caught up in the mistaken idea that business is a game that is played by a set of rules different from what their good sense dictates. They suggest that somehow honesty, truth, and fair play should be set aside when you are talking about business. All is fair in love and war, and business is war! Consequently, some leaders tend to leave their personal moral sense at home, thereby withholding their input on business decisions. Unfortunately, this creates many more cases in which ethical misdeeds occur. This is a fundamental error.

Input from close colleagues

It has often been said that it is lonely at the top of an organization. The person at the top bears the ultimate responsibility for all the important decisions. Some leaders make the job lonelier by excluding the input of those with expertise on the matter under consideration. A good leader must be open to constructive input and criticism and to use this input to make better decisions.

Some businesspeople employ an autocratic managerial style that discourages open communications. As businesses become more global in scope and complexity, getting the information needed to make good decisions assumes greater importance. Expert guidance from those who can provide cross-cultural understanding and insight is vitally important. Without access to all the available information, no wonder leaders can make boneheaded choices.

Deadlines and time pressures

Executives are decision-makers. That's their job. Their day is filled with deciding which issues demand quick action, how to arrange their schedule, how an impending crisis can be averted, whom to see, or what additional information is needed to make a good decision in a specific case. The typical executive makes more than three hundred business decisions each day — that's an average of one every two minutes. Consequently, executives try to prioritize so that they can devote additional time and mental energy to the most important problems. They also save time by taking shortcuts on what they hope are the less important decisions.

Executives may ignore a problem, rely on a subordinate to handle it, or make a gut-level decision without obtaining data. Just as a baseball player doesn't get a hit in every turn at bat, an executive realizes that not every decision will be a good one. But a high batting average would sure be nice! There simply isn't enough time in the day to make a well-considered determination in every situation. This "bias toward action" is an admired trait, but it carries a potentially large downside.

Force for Good

Bernie Ebbers, the CEO and driving force behind the creation of WorldCom, used this defense at his trial. His company had overstated quarterly profits by $3.8 billion, which misled investors and caused WorldCom stock to rise beyond its true market value. Mr. Ebbers maintained that the overstatement of earnings was not his fault. Rather, it was due to deceptions devised by the financial experts whom he had hired and entrusted with managing and reporting the firm's finances. Essentially, he had been too busy to provide oversight regarding their activities and had not asked the right questions that would have uncovered their deceptions. However, ultimate responsibility lies at the top of any organization. Bernie Ebbers was found guilty and was sentenced to twenty-five years in prison.

Organizational culture and practice

A company must develop a culture that supports its values. Developing that culture requires a compliance program. Such a program can be used to ensure fairness and consistency in the handling of ethical issues over time and help educate new employees about expectations and performance standards. This educational component is especially important as workforces become more international or diverse. Employees from different cultural, educational, and family backgrounds need a common understanding so they know what is expected. Compliance programs should be headed by a compliance officer charged with making sure that employees live up to the ideals stated in the code of conduct. Research has shown that organizations with well-defined ethical codes seem to have happier, more-productive employees.[118]

---

[118] Chia-Mei Shih and Chin-Yuan Chen, "The Effect of Organizational Ethical Culture on Marketing Managers' Role Stress

Harvey Seegers, one of my faculty colleagues in the Busch School of Business and Economics, served under Jack Welch at General Electric. Harvey assures me that Jack followed many of the steps toward implementing a culture of integrity that we've just outlined. First, he assessed the company's performance and recognized that a lack of trust was a problem throughout his firm. Then he began implementing a culture of honesty by constantly talking about the need for honesty and by telling employees, "Customers must be able to trust us, and I have to be able to trust you!"

He proactively searched for misconduct anywhere in the company, and often repeated Ronald Reagan's line, "Trust but verify." He gave his corporate audit staff the responsibility to discover policy violations wherever they might be found. Harvey tells me that Jack was a realist, and knew that in a global company with employees from many backgrounds, there was sure to be wrongdoing going on somewhere, sometime. But, its inevitability did not discourage Jack from trying to find it. He placed smart, motivated, ambitious young men and women on the audit staff and challenged them to "find the bad guys where they are hiding."

Although Jack Welch preached integrity, promoted integrity, and tried to implement integrity throughout GE, there was one misconception that threw the proverbial monkey wrench into his actions: a stunted understanding of the principle of human dignity. Putting people first is one of the four core principles of integrity, but Jack didn't act as if he understood that principle completely. Just look at his implementation of the "vitality" curve.

---

and Ethical Behavior Intentions," *Journal of American Academy of Business* 8, no. 1 (March 2006): 89–95.

Jack required that individual managers should be ranked each year according to their performance, and then the bottom 10 percent should be asked to leave in order to make room for new talent. Harvey Seegers said that Jack required GE to take this "bitter pill" so that the organization might undergo continual renewal. Professional sports teams do this type of performance ranking all the time, so why shouldn't businesses do the same?

There are two reasons why this "rank and yank" approach doesn't fit with the human-dignity principle. First, it incorrectly presumes that individual performance is unchangeable and denies an opportunity for improvement. Once you've been rated as a poor performer, you're done. The presumption is that you'll stay a poor performer no matter what you do to try to improve. But is this correct?

Major-league baseball teams send their poor performers to the minors, where problems in hitting or pitching can be ironed out, and once resolved, the players can be recalled later in the season. No employee tries to be a poor performer—that would be contrary to human nature. When given the opportunity to improve, employees usually work to improve what they do. Practice may not make us perfect, but we surely can get better.

Second, because business performance relies so much on employees working together as a team, the overvaluing of individual performance in our rankings means that we might undervalue the effects the individual has on the performance of those around him. Sometimes the poorer performer has certain skills that help make the overall team more cohesive and effective. This aspect of performance is difficult to measure. When employees are fearful of losing their jobs, they are more likely to spend time polishing their own star and less time helping others on the team. Overall team performance can suffer as a result.

When an organization really understands human dignity, it will measure an individual's performance against objective standards, not pit one against another. Further, the organization will establish hiring and management practices to provide the tools, resources, and preparation that enables individual employees to meet the agreed-upon performance standards. This is what we mean by putting people first.

Stakeholder influences

As discussed previously, stakeholders are people who have a stake in the success of the business. Those who put up the investment capital are shareholders and represent one stakeholder group. Other stakeholders include employees, customers, suppliers, and the communities in which businesses locate. All stakeholders should benefit from a healthy, growing business, and the rights and obligations of all these stakeholders should be respected as decisions are made. Good decisions should raise all boats like a rising tide. Poor decisions often favor one group at the expense of another.

Naturally, shareholders are very interested in the financial health and profitability of a firm. The value of their investment increases when earnings increase.

Consequently, through an elected board of directors, they like to apply pressure to the firm to increase profitability sooner rather than later. These short-term objectives are important when they provide benchmarks along the path toward achieving long-term strategic goals. They serve to rally both leadership and employees to achieve concentrated effort and attention. But striving to achieve short-term objectives can backfire, especially if other stakeholder groups are ignored in the process. For instance, a plan to increase profitability (benefiting shareholders) by decreasing employee benefits (adversely affecting employees), or increasing factory emissions (adversely affecting the community around the factory) may not be ethical.

Here's another example. "Chainsaw Al" Dunlap, who earned his nickname by cutting labor and administrative costs from troubled companies, was hired as CEO of Sunbeam Corporation and given the charge to turn around this venerable maker of kitchen appliances. To ensure short-term sales objectives were met, he instituted a "bill and hold" program in which retailers were encouraged to order merchandise for future delivery *and* future payment. These orders were recorded as sales on Sunbeam's income statement, which inflated Sunbeam's reported revenues and profits.

While this practice was technically legal, Dunlap ignored his obligation to inform investors (and the board of directors) about what he was doing. When the "bill and hold" program was finally divulged to investors, some shareholders sued the company, the stock price fell, and every investor's holding lost value. In this case, an action intended to make short-term sales goals to benefit one stakeholder group (employees with sales incentive compensation) adversely impacted another stakeholder group (shareholders). This is not a winning formula!

A more important reason for ethical failure

When you read the stories about Jeffrey Skilling, Kenneth Lay, Dennis Kozlowski, Bernie Ebbers, and Bernie Madoff, do you notice the same thing I do? At the time of their wrongdoing, none of them seemed to have a strong spiritual life. I suspect that a lack of spiritual grounding reduced their resolve to stay on the sound ethical path. That was the overriding reason they committed the acts that got them into trouble.

A lack of spiritual grounding can blind our understanding of right and wrong, close our ears to the advice of others, and make us more sensitive to time pressures. This can alter how we evaluate what is going on around us and twist our analysis in the wrong direction. Each of us needs to cultivate a strong relationship with God through prayer, spiritual reading, and frequent reception of the sacraments. We need divine inspiration and divine strength to be true to the values we hold dear. Without such a relationship, we don't stand a chance.

An often-repeated expression helps put us in the right frame of reference: "Pray as though everything depends on God, but work as though everything depends on you." Some attribute this expression to St. Ignatius and others to St. Augustine. Its sentiment reminds us that earnest prayer will get us divine guidance, but we serve as God's instruments, and we can't sit back and expect that God will do everything for us.

Earlier in my career I behaved as if the first line of the expression was missing. Sure, I went to church on Sunday, but that was the full extent of my spiritual life. Fortunately, people and events that God put into my life helped me understand that I wasn't the one who was in control. After several of my decisions blew up in my face, I realized that His way is much better than my way. Now I try to take advantage of all the opportunities that the Church offers for a deepening of faith. As a result, I have a much better relationship with the Lord. I encourage you to do the same.

Using the ethical decision-making framework

Let's look at an example of ethical decision-making using the framework. As a young engineer, I perfected the ability to measure the cycle times of manufacturing operations without the use of a stopwatch. This was an advantageous skill, since factory employees usually get nervous when someone pulls out a stopwatch and begins timing them. With my timing talent, I could walk through the factory and eyeball the speed of every assembly line to see if it was running at the designed rate. And I could do all of this without ever referring to a timing device.

What was my secret? My pulse rate was invariably sixty beats per minute. I could observe a manufacturing operation while counting silently to myself in time with my heartbeat while the machine cycled. If I counted to six, I knew that the cycle time was six seconds, and the rate was ten cycles per minute. If the design rate was supposed to be higher, I could immediately investigate what was going wrong.

Several managers in my company were impressed with my skill. In fact, one manager wanted me to engage in some industrial espionage by traveling to our competitors' plants, identifying myself as a tourist, getting a tour of the plant, and measuring all the cycle times while there. In this way, I could obtain data that would help us benchmark their manufacturing costs and operating efficiency.

It was the manufacturing director's call as to whether I should go on this "undercover" assignment. If he had followed the framework we've been discussing, he would first look at the decision through the lens of his own personal standards of right and wrong. No doubt, he would also relate the idea to our organization's standards and culture. This would include assessing whether the trip put people first, activated personal responsibility, enhanced teamwork, and represented good stewardship of resources.

If he was still concerned, he would next ask trusted colleagues their opinion of the idea, and consider what stakeholders—board members, customers, suppliers, and employees—might think, should they find out about the scheme. Priorities, urgency, and time pressures also would figure into the decision.

In the end, he correctly chose to nix the idea. After all, he understood that good ends don't justify deceptive means.

What happens when ethical decision-making is unethical?

When business leaders make poor ethical decisions, there are adverse consequences that impact the businessperson, the organization, and society as a whole. After a poor ethical decision is made, it may be a long time before any adverse consequence is apparent. This time lag may provide a false sense of security and increase the business practitioner's willingness to continue making decisions with the same shortcomings. When the adverse consequence finally arrives, as it surely will, a whole string of poor ethical behaviors must be evaluated. This exacerbates the problems created and increases the financial and organizational costs in correcting any problems. Look at the VW case (see "The 'Defeat Device' Scam at Volkswagen").

The personal costs of ethical violations among leaders in American corporations should not be minimized. Guilty verdicts can profoundly alter the personal lives of executives, tear apart their families, and ruin their financial wealth. Court cases can drag on for many years and consume fortunes in legal expenses. Unethical actions by leaders at the top of the firm can infect entire organizations, encouraging others to mimic the behaviors, and can result in the loss of resources, in decreased employment levels and consumer and investor confidence, and in bankruptcy. Finally, society is injured severely when others in society emulate the unethical actions of businesspeople, and unethical behavior

The "Defeat Device" Scam at Volkswagen

"We've totally screwed up!" exclaimed Volkswagen America boss Michael Horn.

"We've broken the trust of our customers and the public," said VW group's chief executive, Martin Winterkorn. Winterkorn resigned shortly thereafter.

What were they talking about? The U.S. Environmental Protection Agency had just discovered that VW diesel-engine cars were fitted with software that could detect when emissions testing was being performed and change the engine's performance so that it appeared to meet emission standards. VW admitted that this "defeat device" software was included in more than eleven million vehicles sold worldwide, including the Jetta, the Beetle, the Golf, the Passat, and the Audi A3. In real-life driving, these vehicles belched out nitrogen-oxide pollutants at a rate forty times higher than the emission standards allowed.

Integrity requires that businesses provide goods that are truly good. Deliberate misrepresentation of a product's essential capabilities is not only immoral and unethical but downright criminal. Unethical behavior can have a devastating impact on innocent people:

- Thousands of Volkswagen employees have incurred layoffs due to reduced demand for VW vehicles. Similar layoffs may continue at suppliers as their production diminishes due to lower demand for Volkswagen cars.

- Volkswagen customers own a "stranded asset"
  —an automobile that almost no one wants. Re-
  calling them and replacing them with a comply-
  ing vehicle doesn't fully cover the owner's loss.
- Volkswagen dealers are in possession of stale in-
  ventory—even loss-leading pricing will likely
  not get the cars off the lot.
- As stock prices tumble, Volkswagen investors
  have lost a large portion of their stock value.
- Volkswagen's loss of business could negatively
  impact the German economy, and perhaps the
  entire European economy.
- All of society is breathing dirtier air because of
  the added pollution of eleven million noncom-
  plying vehicles.*

*Harvey Seegers (2015), "The Volkswagen Lessons
in Business Ethics and Leadership," Busch School of
Business and Economics Blog, October 21st, http://
blog.business.cua.edu/2015/10/the-volkswagen-les-
sons-in-business.html.

becomes more widespread throughout industry, entertainment,
institutions, and government.

There are significant benefits to good ethical decision-making. First and foremost, many research studies have confirmed
what should be obvious—that there is a positive and significant
relationship between organization ethicality and organization
performance. Companies that implement an integrity program

are more apt to stay out of legal trouble than those companies that don't. Companies that treat customers, employees, suppliers, or society unethically are not successful long term. They can fool people for a short while, but eventually ethical violations are uncovered and the glare of adverse public opinion takes its toll.

We've reviewed how ethical decision-making takes place, and we've highlighted some of the ways it can go awry. We've also identified how ethical problems, when allowed to happen, can have serious consequences for individuals, businesses, and society. In the next chapter, we'll look at the steps you should take to put your business on a sound ethical footing, a footing that champions all the components of business integrity.

Questions for reflection

1. Think about an organization you know well. Have you ever observed ethical malfeasance in this organization? What happened?

2. Using the Framework for Ethical Decision-Making presented in this chapter, speculate on the cause of the ethical problem you identified in question 1. Can you estimate how much the ethical malfeasance cost the organization?

3. According to the framework, stakeholders can influence the ethicality of decision-making within an organization. Select a company that sells consumer-related products. As a customer, how might you influence that company's decision-making?

4. What must individuals do to keep from living a "divided life," in which they leave their personal character and values at home and just go with the flow at work, even if actions aren't ethical?

5. How's your spiritual life? Do you have a close connection with God, or do you remain at a distance and try to control your life without His help? How can you improve your relationship?

Chapter 9

Creating an Integrity-Infused Organization

O beautiful for heroes proved in liberating strife,
Who more than self their country loved and mercy more than life!
America! America! May God thy gold refine,
Till all success be nobleness, and every gain divine!

—From Katharine Lee Bates, "America the Beautiful"

Professional golfer Wendy Ward won four times on the Ladies Professional Golf Association (LPGA) Tour and made more than $3 million in her career, but perhaps she is best known for the way she lost the 2000 LPGA championship. On the thirteenth hole, Ward called a one-stroke penalty on herself when, after she had already taken a stance over an eight-foot par putt and grounded her putter, the ball moved slightly. Even though Ward never touched the ball, and even though the ball's movement was so slight that nobody would have noticed had she gone through with the putt, the penalty stroke proved to be the margin between her and winner Juli Inkster.

Professional golf has witnessed many wonderful stories of truth, honor, and character in which competitors have called penalties on themselves for rule infractions that no one else would have observed. Bobby Jones, Tom Watson, Phil Mickelson, and Jack

Force for Good

Nicklaus are among the golfing greats who have placed honesty and integrity above winning. The actions of these champions give us the inspiration and confidence that winners can and should have integrity. But how does this come about? As a business professional, how can you develop an organization in which every employee pro-actively follows high standards of integrity? How can you establish a culture in which employees make the right choice whether or not they think someone is watching over their shoulder?

Integrity requires that an effective compliance program is present to ensure that all understand the organization's values, support mechanisms, and code of conduct. In this chapter, we will examine the steps that you can take to make integrity second nature for all your employees. When you do this, your business will become a force for good.

Ten steps to ensuring integrity

An organization with integrity does not happen by chance, and the adoption of codes of ethics, by itself, is not a complete strat-egy. We've seen some companies adopt codes of ethics and then promptly ignore every rule in the code!

Integrity is the result of a conscious effort to make sure that everyone is on the same page. Although some companies have implemented integrity programs that are little more than window dressing, ostensibly to deflect attention and culpability resulting from illegal actions, these approaches ultimately serve no one. The serious organization should implement all ten steps, as these actions provide an underlying structure that can be adapted to meet the needs of various businesses. All are necessary to estab-lish and maintain a good ethical climate and reduce the number of incidents of ethical malfeasance.

Creating an Integrity-Infused Organization

Ten Steps to Develop Integrity in Your Organization

1. Pray	Begin by getting your own prayer life in order, then invite others in your organization to do the same. Initiate group prayer (or at the minimum, a moment of silence) before meetings.
2. Self-Assess	Identify company values, shortcomings, and elements of any integrity program already in place. Identify priority areas where there is greater risk that ethical difficulties may occur.
3. Establish Standards	Establish clear standards and procedures that apply to all employees, and make these readily available.
4. Ensure Commitment	Delegate the responsibility for overseeing compliance to a specific high-level manager. Make commitment part of the compensation package. Ensure that senior management demonstrates its dedication to the program.
5. Recruit	Ensure that new hires have good moral character and sound ethical preparation.
6. Train	Provide timely training that helps employees know rules and values. Build employee capacity to exercise moral judgment.

7. Communicate	Provide correspondence and reference materials that explain the requirements. Identify what must be repeated for effectiveness. Use multiple channels to reinforce the message.
8. Support	Provide confidential resources to which employees can go with problems and concerns. Make sure these resources are reliable and trusted.
9. Enforce	Determine how violations will be investigated, violators sanctioned, and appeals conducted. Ensure that processes work smoothly and efficiently, and roles and responsibilities are clear.
10. Improve	Continually improve the process. When violations are detected, the organization must take steps to respond and to prevent further violations.

1. Pray

Prayer should be the first step on any list. Prayer is an essential dialogue with God in which we thank Him for His blessings, share our hopes and concerns, and then listen for His guidance. Once you get your prayer life in order, you can work toward getting others in your organization to do the same. When two or more are gathered together in prayer, the prayer becomes exceptionally powerful.

I joined the Catholic University of America because of an opportunity to help create a different kind of business school — one that integrated faith and reason into the study of business. Creating a new business school is not something that happens very often these days, and we knew we needed help.

Our first step was to storm heaven with our prayers. We began attending daily Mass and doing acts of penance. One of our benefactors gave us a large statue of St. Michael, and we placed it in our main office and began saying the St. Michael prayer each day.

The formation of the school was approved by the university's board of trustees and announced in a *Wall Street Journal* article on January 8, 2013. That was the same day that I was diagnosed with a virulent form of cancer and told that I had, at most, three years to live.

I don't know about you, but being diagnosed with cancer seemed to me to be the worst thing that could happen to anyone. My wife and I received some good advice from a priest friend, who recommended that we print up some Archbishop Fulton Sheen prayer cards and send them to friends and relatives, asking them to join us in prayer. Meanwhile, I offered my suffering as penance to help build up our new school and resigned myself to getting something significant accomplished in the time I had left.

People from all over the world began praying for me and for our school. I was able to work for two more years while I underwent treatment until the pain and an inability to stand required me to take a leave of absence. By January 2015, my kidneys were shutting down, and I was close to death. Then I was given a new medication, and suddenly I began improving. Just three months later—Holy Thursday, 2015—I got the news that I was cancer free! Prayer helped me throughout this whole ordeal, and I know it will help you as well.

Individual prayer is important, and so is group prayer. Group prayer before meetings can be a powerful way to center business colleagues' thinking about issues under discussion. A number of organizations that I've worked with, including those with secular orientations, followed a discipline of beginning meetings with an invocation for God's help. This can take the form of a moment of silence, or a standard nondenominational prayer, or even a series of denominational prayers led by individuals who take their turn from meeting to meeting. Even though we don't all agree on the best way to worship, we do tend to agree on the need to invoke God's assistance. When it is done right, most people appreciate this moment of workplace prayer.

2. Conduct rigorous self-assessment

Before determining how to implement integrity into its business, a company must take stock of its current situation. This requires a self-assessment of its values, shortcomings, culture, organizational structure, and the special nature of its business. The self-assessment process should provide ample opportunity for every employee to participate and identify his or her perceptions of the current ethical climate of the organization. You don't want to sugarcoat the analysis. You need to know all of your organization's concerns and imperfections so that the compliance program you implement will address all of your needs.

The self-assessment should identify priority areas, where there is greater risk that problems may occur. For instance, if the firm is frequently involved in securing contracts in foreign countries, perhaps bribery or other violations of the Foreign Corrupt Practices Act should be identified as a priority area. As a result of the assessment, the business should have a full understanding of what elements of any existing ethical compliance program can be retained and what needs to be created anew.

3. Create and communicate a written code

In this step, the organization should establish clear compliance standards and procedures for all stakeholders, and make these standards readily available. Firms have referred to these standards by different names, including codes of integrity, codes of conduct, codes of ethics, or statements of values. Whatever you call it, your code should include guiding principles, a list of ethical and unethical types of behavior, and procedures for reporting violations.

There are three objectives to keep in mind. First, communicate to all those associated with the organization that the purpose of your code is not just to avoid prosecution, but rather to promote principled behavior by everyone involved. Second, the code itself should be more than a simple catalog of offenses and punishments; it should provide overall direction, guidance, and encouragement to promote right behavior. Third, the code should use clear, unambiguous language that can be understood by all concerned.

Your code should reflect uniform compliance with the values, rules, and policies that the firm has adopted. This would include the core integrity principles of human dignity, solidarity, subsidiarity, and the common good, as well as the exercise of the most important virtues for your business. Some firms also incorporate biblical principles into their code, such as honesty, excellence, personal responsibility, commitment, compassion, citizenship, respect for others and their property, and fairness. (See "LaVallee's Dozen: Twelve Values We Live By.")

Merely having standards is not enough. A company must make the standards understood and ensure their dissemination throughout the organization. Remember that standards do not address every possible issue that will be encountered in daily

LaVallee's Dozen: Twelve Values We Live By

1. *Trust and respect* for people at all levels. Let honesty and integrity guide your words and actions. Every encounter with workers, vendors, suppliers, and customers is a new opportunity to build trust and foster loyalty.

2. *Teamwork* that supports the efforts of your associates and encourages them to do their best. You can run with the ball, but it takes a team to win the game.

3. *Empowerment* to make a difference, no matter what your role is in the organization. Take initiative, make decisions, and demonstrate leadership.

4. *Personal growth* as you help grow the company. Own the company vision, and share your views. Your concerns and opinions matter to everyone in the organization.

5. *Optimism* about your job that energizes others. Enthusiasm is contagious, so take pride in your work, be cheerful, and have fun.

6. *Customer service* that always exceeds customer expectations. Think "yes" and go the extra mile to make it happen. Let a smile be your calling card with every customer interaction.

7. *Commitment* to doing great work, regardless of obstacles. It is the key to your success, and the success of the company.

8. *Dependability* to customers and coworkers alike. Be prompt, courteous, and respectful of others' time.

9. *Quality* is everyone's responsibility. The impression you make on customers and vendors is a lasting one and reflects the company's image.

10. *Efficiency* in our operations adds value to everything we do. Our number-one goal is to make it easy for customers to do business with us.

11. *Preparation and presentation* of what we make, what we do, and who we are. Your words, actions, and appearance determine our reputation and our success.

12. *Safety* begins with you. Keep our facilities and equipment neat, clean, and in safe working order. Use equipment with care and be mindful of others.*

*Courtesy of LaVallee's Bakery, Boston, Massachusetts.

operations, but they do help employees resolve ethical dilemmas by prescribing or limiting certain activities. Standards should communicate what is expected of employees and prescribe penalties for any violation.

I recommend that your standards be printed and given to all employees, not simply posted on a website or bulletin board. Handing out standards in writing underscores their importance and encourages employees to read them, learn them, and comply with them.

4. Ensure Commitment

The fourth step in creating an integrity-infused business is for the CEO to obtain commitment from all levels of the organization, especially senior management and the board of directors. If there is pushback, managers should attempt to find out and address the reasons for employee nonacceptance. A positive ethical climate is necessary, or compliance will be seen as one more job task rather than as a way of life. If the top of the organization merely pays lip service to the plan, employees will view the plan as unimportant and burdensome. Accordingly, the CEO must be seen as an uncompromising proponent of good ethical behavior and a champion of compliance.

The responsibility for implementing integrity should be entrusted to a specific high-level executive or "compliance officer" who has high personal ethical standards and a participatory leadership style. Rest assured that responsibility must be matched with authority. At the same time, the compliance officer and the oversight committee should be mentors and coaches, not autocrats or dictators. Micromanagement and commands issued "on high" can create the wrong kind of ethical environment, so that employees act to avoid sanctions rather than act with good ethical reasoning. Management discussions and announcements should support an organization culture that infuses these positions with moral legitimacy.

Gaining real commitment by employees should be made part of the compensation packages for all supervisors. Furthermore, each employee job description should include requirements to identify potential ethical problems in that employee's area and to achieve ethical outcomes consistent with the values of the organization. Consider how the CEO of The Wine Group takes an active part in assuring integrity (see "Developing Cultural Values at The Wine Group, Inc.").

Developing Cultural Values at The Wine Group, Inc.

Art Ciocca drew a simple figure on the whiteboard. It was a teeter-totter. He wrote "politics" on one end and "performance" on the other. Then he explained, "Many companies make their decisions based on expediency and maximizing short-term returns each quarter so that some company VP earns an incentive bonus. That's doing the political thing, and that's not what we do in our company. Instead, we focus on doing the right thing today, tomorrow, and every day so that we create long-term value. That's what we mean by performance."

At the time, Art was CEO of The Wine Group and had just led a group of colleagues in a leveraged-buyout of the firm. His teeter-totter speech was being delivered to a group of new employees.

"Notice what happens when companies waste their time and resources on the political thing," he said as he redrew the teeter-totter so that the "politics" side was higher. "The amount of effort spent on performance goes down," he continued. "Here's what we want," he said, and he redrew the teeter-totter so that the "performance" side was raised all the way up.

From its beginning, the company adopted a long-term posture in the highly cyclical wine business. The founding documents even refer to the key people not as managers or directors but as stewards. Art's team never set out deliberately to develop a set of cultural values, but company values developed as the team wrestled with problems and learned to work together. Surely they were influenced by the family values they learned growing up, but ultimately the values they adopted for the company were developed from experiencing mistakes and successes in the business. The Wine Group's Ten Core Cultural Values are these:

1. Offering the best consumer value
2. Putting performance first and eliminating politics
3. Encouraging everyone to take a proprietary interest in his or her work
4. Keeping it simple—continually reducing complex problems to simple solutions
5. Maintaining flexibility to deal with agricultural events and to capitalize on changing marketplace opportunities
6. Exercising entrepreneurial risk-taking
7. Thinking outside the box to innovate and to solve problems
8. Operating with the highest integrity because good ethics are good business
9. Being proud but never arrogant
10. Being good stewards of the gifts given

As a result of their adherence to these values over the years, The Wine Group has grown from a failing business into one of the largest wine producers in the world. Its Franzia brand ranks among the top sellers in the U.S. market.*

*Based on an interview with Art Ciocca, March 29, 2017.

5. Recruit employees with good moral character

Naturally, an organization must start with employees who have a well-developed sense of ethics and a strong moral compass. If you begin with an organization full of liars, cheats, and scoundrels, you'll have a very difficult task ahead! The character and level of moral development of prospective employees should be assessed during the interview process, and only those prospects who demonstrate high moral character should be considered for hire.

As highlighted in the accompanying story (see "Hiring for Virtue at Koch Industries"), Koch Industries is one organization that is successful in hiring for character. You can do the same in your business. When character is emphasized during the hiring process, all employees get the message that character is important and the organization takes good character seriously.

6. Ensure that all employees have the opportunity to grow in integrity

Continuous improvement should be your goal. All employees must become knowledgeable about organizational values and standards, and build a capacity to exercise moral judgment.

Hiring for Virtue at Koch Industries

Charles Koch, CEO of Koch Industries, is quick to point out that his firm implements a different approach to hiring. In his book, *Good Profit*, he describes it this way: "While some companies focus exclusively on hiring individuals with the requisite skills for their openings and then hope these recruits possess aligned values, Koch transposes that approach. We focus *first* on values."

The company's experience suggests that new hires with the right values invariably make better employees. That's why the company screens all applicants for good character starting with the first contact. Recruiters inquire into candidates' past behavior regarding integrity, compliance, value creation, and other of the firm's guiding principles. They listen for behaviors such as how candidates have dealt with difficult situations, whether they are respectful when speaking about others, whether they are bureaucratic, or if they have difficulty admitting mistakes.

When a candidate is selected for on-site interviews, the recruiter, hiring manager, and interviewers conduct one-on-one discussions to determine whether a candidate is aligned across all of the company's ten guiding principles. This discipline has greatly improved the firm's ability to select high-performing, long-term employees who behave in a manner consistent with company values.

"An employee with great talent but bad values can do far more damage to a company than an employee with good values," explained Charles Koch. "Our experience shows that employees with good values can gain the required skills and knowledge to become outstanding employees through on-the-job training."*

*Koch, *Good Profit*, pp. 132–134.

But more than that, all employees should participate in helping the business identify and capitalize on areas for improvement. Initial training for new employees can be conducted in stand-alone programs that run for an hour or two, but to be most effective, employees need to understand that part of their job is to help the business improve. Gathering employees together periodically to work toward understanding what a particular virtue means in practice, how well the firm exhibits that virtue, and how it might improve its effectiveness can help make integrity an ongoing organizational commitment.

Training sessions should be structured to help awaken all employees' desires to do right. Enhancing individual abilities to recognize ethical situations will increase the frequency with which employees make moral considerations and use moral reasoning. Training should encourage improved moral sensitivity, improved moral decision-making, and the development of virtues such as integrity and courage as they apply in a business setting. Employees should be schooled in how to analyze and judge a situation based on relevant ethical principles, acting out of choice rather than out of fear.

Sessions should not focus merely on memorization of policies or laws; rather, situations, role-playing, and personal stories should be included. The training should model the right behaviors in addition to calling attention to wrong behaviors. The social norms of the organization are perceived as a powerful influence on the ethicality of individuals; and role-playing and case studies, especially those that show employees doing the right thing, help clarify and emphasize social norms. Practical scenarios in which employees can test their ethical knowledge and real-world examples and situations that are relevant to employees' jobs help drive home ethical concepts. Finally, giving individual employees the opportunity to lead training sessions can be very effective.

Some companies exempt executives from legal and ethical training that is compulsory for other employees. This exemption should be avoided since it sends the signal that the company is delivering the training because it is required to, rather than because it is a fundamental, respected company value.

7. Provide consistent communication

Step 7 is to provide consistent, ongoing communications to all stakeholder groups—employees, customers, suppliers, investors, and the communities in which the organization has operations. Correspondence and reference materials should be distributed to explain the program and its requirements for all. Some organizations include handbooks, wall posters, signs, wallet cards, newsletters, annual reports, company magazines, and websites as part of their multifaceted communications efforts. Managers should be cognizant that repetition is appropriate in any good communications campaign.

The most important component of any integrity program is senior management's continued public commitment to it. All the training in the world won't help if the company leaders don't live it. It must be regularly apparent on the lips and pens of executives. The integrity message must be communicated in a variety of ways with regular frequency.

8. Provide confidential resources

Most employees are reluctant to accuse fellow employees of ethical wrongdoing in an open forum. If given a private and confidential chance to convey information or to ask questions about ethical practices they observe, however, they will readily do so. Consequently, organizations should provide confidential resources where employees can go with problems and concerns. These resources must be perceived to be reliable and trusted by employees. The compliance officer might be the first choice.

9. Respond and enforce consistently, promptly, and fairly

The ninth step is to determine how ethical violations will be investigated, how violators will be sanctioned, and how appeals will be conducted. The requirements are meaningless unless everyone understands what disciplinary mechanisms will be followed to enforce the requirements. Enforcement should involve punishment of the perpetrator. Termination or legal action, or both, may be deserved and help protect the organization from future ethical lapses. Justice requires that an appeal process also be provided.

Processes should work smoothly and efficiently, and roles and responsibilities should be clear and well documented. Once the organization has had a few years of consistent results, however, there may be a tendency to let down the guard a little. Managers may get lulled into a false sense of security and adopt the attitude that the integrity compliance program is up and running and we need to devote our attention to other business challenges. When the program is ignored, however, ethical lapses often occur.

To keep the organization from lapsing into a false sense of ethical security, the compliance program must be continually audited and monitored, and feedback must be provided from and to employees. Unfortunately, there is a temptation for individuals responsible for reporting to lose sight of the purpose of such activities, which is to identify any weaknesses in ethical conduct and to correct them so that the organization can improve over time. Human-resource professionals should track the number of employee grievance complaints and evaluate employee responses to ethical-attitude surveys. Another way to assess whether the integrity program is working is to include integrity questions on employee exit interviews.

10. Make continuous improvements

The last step in the process is to strive for continuous improvement, which should be based on employee feedback and participation. Employees should be allowed to voice their opinions about the nature and effect of the code of conduct, the integrity of officials, the delegation of authority, the communication and training programs, and the auditing activities.

When violations are detected, the organization should take steps to respond and to prevent further violations. Filling out forms, drafting carefully crafted policies, and producing lists of employees who have undergone training courses will not, in and of themselves, improve things.

A company should build a culture that encourages commitment to the law and to good ethical sense. Employees should know, for example, that no matter what the issue is and who is involved, deception, lying, fabricating records, or covering up problems is unacceptable. The standard of conduct is stated, applied, repeated, and understood by everyone in the organization, regardless of job title or tenure.

While the headlines focus on major indictable offenses, such as insider trading and corruption, most ethical infractions aren't so obvious. Smaller, often inconspicuous actions, such as personal use of company property, can foster an environment where ethical errors multiply. Continuously seeking out and correcting these minor violations will help the organization avoid future major lapses.

How important is leadership?

Several years ago a Coca-Cola Company employee and two accomplices attempted to sell trade secrets to rival Pepsi-Cola.[119] According to the story, one of the accomplices sent a letter to Pepsi, claiming to be a high-placed Coca-Cola official who was willing to sell confidential documents and new-product samples for the right price. Pepsi exercised appropriate ethical leadership by promptly turning over the letter and envelope to Coca-Cola's CEO, who contacted the FBI. An FBI undercover agent posed as a Pepsi executive and contacted the trio, negotiating a deal to purchase documents and a sample of product under laboratory development for $1.5 million. Surveillance photography caught the perpetrators on tape as they stole the documents and samples. All three were arrested the day the exchange was to be made.

Ethical leadership is not preaching, or the uttering of pieties, or the insistence on social conformity. Ethical leadership

---

[119] Kathleen Kingsbury, "You Can't Beat the Real Thing," *Time*, vol. 168, no. 3, July 17, 2006, pp. 9–10.

is responding correctly and decisively when an ethical dilemma emerges. When the trade-secret-offer letter arrived at Pepsi, at least one executive recognized that Pepsi's code of integrity required fair treatment of competitors, and this executive responded correctly by sending the offer letter to Coca-Cola management. Pepsi spokesperson Dave DeCecco explained, "Competition can be fierce, but competition must also be fair and legal."

The ethical leader is characterized by high ideals and a strong sense of duty, by a strong drive for task completion, and for both vigor and persistence in pursuit of ethical goals. The ethical leader is self-confident and willing to accept consequences of decision and action and has the capacity to structure social interaction to good purpose. It takes true leadership to implement integrity across the organization.

Leadership is always associated with attainment of group objectives and implies activity, movement, and getting work done. A leader occupies a position of responsibility in coordinating the activities of the members of a group in their task of attaining a common goal. The personal characteristics of the leader must bear some relevant relationship to the characteristics, activities, and goals of the followers. If not, the followers will have difficulty identifying with the leader and in following his or her lead.

The personal ethical standards of the leader have a very strong influence on the ethical behavior of others in the organization. Leaders need to have a well-formed conscience and self-confidence in expressing their views in order to inspire others to follow their ethical lead.

Organizational culture and practices have a huge impact on continuing ethical behavior, and consequently, a leader must work to establish a culture of integrity among employees. The development of respect for legal and ethical standards across the organization requires a leader who does his or her homework. That leader needs an understanding of the law as a minimal threshold and a commitment to establish higher ethical norms, train employees, assess results, and seek continuous improvement. This requires outstanding ethical leadership at the top of the organization.

Now it's *your* turn!

We know that businesspeople often need basic guidance and education so that they increase their "batting average" in making good ethical decisions. There are standards of performance that are discernable, make good business sense, and will assist everyone in making better decisions. With your confidence high, you are now ready to take over and guide others.

Remember that your personal ethical standards can and should have a significant influence on the business decisions that you make. That's the starting point. Just as an organization is an extension of individual action, business ethics is an extension of personal ethics. What is right and what is wrong is consistent whether we are dealing with individual or organizational action.

As we've seen, ethical missteps can lead to criminal convictions and imprisonment for executives, business failures, and significant loss of financial resources for shareholders. Organizations with integrity can be more secure and more successful over the long term than organizations without standards. Insisting on high ethical standards improves employee morale and increases both recruitment and retention. Organizations that establish a reputation of fairness and ethical behavior will attract outstanding employees who will want to work for them and will attract other great companies that will want to collaborate. The result is win-win.

Whether the practice of business is truly a profession has long been debated.[120] The traditional definition requires that members of a "profession" must "profess" that they will conduct themselves uprightly and uphold certain moral and ethical standards.[121] Since business has no formal standards of conduct and since business practitioners are not required to uphold specified moral standards, some argue that business should not be called a profession.

But I disagree. The standards of integrity that we've been discussing in this book qualify as well-founded standards of right and wrong, standards that make human interaction fruitful. When business professionals resolve to uphold them, what they practice is not only a noble vocation, but a noble profession as well.

This chapter began with lines taken from the third verse of "America the Beautiful," the uplifting song written by Katharine Lee Bates. The last line speaks to each one of us working in this profession we call business. When we tackle difficult problems, when we bring people together to accomplish good things, and when we work to build organizations with integrity, we are drawn to a further exaltation of good character, ideals, and virtuous conduct. The successes we achieve can be noble and our undertakings can receive the blessings of God. The world can truly become a better place for all. Paraphrasing Katharine, all of our

---

[120] Louis D. Brandeis, "Business as a Profession" (address delivered at Brown University Commencement, 1912).

[121] Richard Barker, "The Big Idea: No, Management Is Not a Profession," *Harvard Business Review* (July–August 2010).

success will be the result of nobleness, and every gain will be divine.

After reading this book, you have the understanding necessary to implement integrity into your organization and guide others. Now is the time for action. I wish you the best of success. I pray that you and your business will be a force for good in this world!

Questions for reflection

1. Suppose your friend started a business and adopted the Golden Rule as the business's code of integrity. Do you believe the Golden Rule would be sufficient to guide employees to integrity? What would you recommend?

2. Do any of the businesses you are familiar with screen for moral character when they recruit? What types of questions would you ask to get a handle on an applicant's character?

3. If you were charged with developing activities and programs for employees that help improve the integrity of the firm, what might you include?

About the Author

Dr. Brian Engelland is ordinary professor of marketing in the Busch School of Business and Economics at the Catholic University of America. He holds the Edward J. Pryzbyla Chair of Business and Economics.

Dr. Engelland's research focuses on how marketing executives process inputs in deciding how to market products and services. Naturally, this involves investigation into the personal ethics, virtue, and religiousness of the marketing decision-maker. Dr. Engelland has authored more than seventy refereed publications and six books, has won multiple teaching awards, and has been named a fellow of the Marketing Management Association. In 2013 he received the Society for Marketing Advances Lifetime Contributor to Marketing Award.

Prior to becoming an academic, Dr. Engelland was a product development executive and served in a series of leadership positions for two Fortune 500 corporations. Later he became president of a marketing consultancy agency, Engelland and Associates, which helped clients successfully introduce new products and services across the globe.

Dr. Engelland holds a bachelor's degree from Purdue University, an MBA from the University of Cincinnati, and a doctorate from Southern Illinois University. Before joining the faculty at Catholic University, he served as marketing department head at Mississippi State University. He and his wife, Barbara, have three children and eight grandchildren. Engelland is a Fourth Degree Knight of Columbus and a Knight Commander with Star in the Equestrian Order of the Holy Sepulchre of Jerusalem.

THE CATHOLIC UNIVERSITY OF AMERICA
THE BUSCH SCHOOL OF BUSINESS AND ECONOMICS

We believe that our professional expertise and our commitment to Catholic Social Doctrine make us uniquely capable of applying Church teachings on business and economics in ways that can be broadly adopted, practical, and effective for organizations and society today.

The Busch School of Business and Economics seeks to transform the world of business, believing that:

- The human person is at the center of the economy.
- Business is a noble vocation.
- Business can be a force for good.
- Business advances human flourishing through the alleviation of poverty and the inherent dignity found in work.

Our focus on business as a force for good, always benefitting the human person, is one that can be understood and embraced by people of all faiths.

Our school has a very clear mission: to help the business world understand how to implement Catholic Social Doctrine in a way that benefits businesses, the people they employ, and society as a whole.

The Catholic Church has developed a rich and deeply rooted body of thought about economic and social justice over more than a hundred years. Recently, Pope Francis has reached out to businesspeople asking us to find new ways to create jobs and encourage entrepreneurship. Calling business a "noble vocation," the pope has challenged business professionals and economists to work to build organizations and economies that are sustainable, just, and beneficial to all.

The Busch School of Business and Economics at the Catholic University of America serves to provide thought-leading undergraduate and graduate-level education and scholarship in business and economics informed by the Catholic social principles of human dignity, solidarity, subsidiarity, and the common good.

These principles of Catholic Social Doctrine are not opposed to capitalism or a free-market economy. On the contrary, they are practical, helpful, visionary guidelines about how to use resources and build organizations that will enable individuals and societies to flourish within a free economy.

We integrate these principles into all aspects of business—accounting, economics, finance, management, marketing, and so forth—in a way that does not diminish academic and professional excellence, but rather lifts the whole enterprise to a higher level. It is an innovative, entrepreneurial, and rigorous approach to teaching business and economics. Our students and graduates are living proof that it works, inspiring achievement both in the classroom and in the workplace.

It is a great benefit for our students to be located in Washington, D.C.: internships, exposure to top-level business and economic leaders, and the job opportunities that abound in this area all give the Busch School of Business and Economics an added competitive advantage.

The students, faculty, and staff of the Busch School of Business and Economics are striving to grow as persons of integrity and virtue as we apply professional knowledge and skills to the goal of transforming the world of business into a force for good. We invite you to become part of this exciting and inspiring enterprise.

More information is available at business.catholic.edu.

Index

Index

Index

Index

Sophia Institute

Sophia Institute is a nonprofit institution that seeks to nurture the spiritual, moral, and cultural life of souls and to spread the Gospel of Christ in conformity with the authentic teachings of the Roman Catholic Church.

Sophia Institute Press fulfills this mission by offering translations, reprints, and new publications that afford readers a rich source of the enduring wisdom of mankind.

Sophia Institute also operates two popular online Catholic resources: CrisisMagazine.com and CatholicExchange.com.

Crisis Magazine provides insightful cultural analysis that arms readers with the arguments necessary for navigating the ideological and theological minefields of the day. *Catholic Exchange* provides world news from a Catholic perspective as well as daily devotionals and articles that will help you to grow in holiness and live a life consistent with the teachings of the Church.

In 2013, Sophia Institute launched Sophia Institute for Teachers to renew and rebuild Catholic culture through service to Catholic education. With the goal of nurturing the spiritual, moral, and cultural life of souls, and an abiding respect for the role and work of teachers, we strive to provide materials and programs that are at once enlightening to the mind and ennobling to the heart; faithful and complete, as well as useful and practical.

Sophia Institute gratefully recognizes the Solidarity Association for preserving and encouraging the growth of our apostolate over the course of many years. Without their generous and timely support, this book would not be in your hands.

www.SophiaInstitute.com
www.CatholicExchange.com
www.CrisisMagazine.com
www.SophiaInstituteforTeachers.org